The
START-UP of YOU

REID HOFFMAN is co-founder and chairman of LinkedIn, the biggest professional social network in the world with 100+ million members. Previously he was executive vice president of PayPal. He is also a partner at Greylock, a leading Silicon Valley venture capital firm. He has been an early investor in over 100 technology companies, including Facebook and Zynga.

BEN CASNOCHA is an award-winning entrepreneur and author. He has written for Newsweek and appeared on CNN, the CBS Early Show and Fox News. BusinessWeek named him one of 'America's best young entrepreneurs' and he is in much demand as a public speaker.

Praise for The START-UP of YOU

'Everyone, women and men alike, needs to think big to succeed. This is a practical book that shows you how to take control and build a career that will enable you to have real impact.'

–SHERYL SANDBERG, Chief Operating Officer, Facebook

'Silicon Valley revolutionizes entire industries through the way we work. It is now time to export our playbook to the rest of the world. *The Start-up of You* is that key playbook: it will help you revolutionize yourself and achieve your own career breakout.'

–MARC ANDREESSEN, co-founder Netscape; director at HP, Facebook, and eBay

'Rather than containing the usual tranche of aphorisms and advice on how to create lists of things you want to achieve, *The Start-up of You* suggests arranging your career like a business ... We challenge you not to be inspired'

–*PA Life*

'The most compelling parts of this book are the ones that look at the importance of developing and exploiting professional networks. As well as explaining network intelligence, or why your contacts' contact may be the best source of leads about potential jobs, the book also gives numerous tips – including ones gleaned from the world of online dating – about how best to broker effective relationships'

–Economist

'It is the optimism of Silicon Valley that infuses this book: there is still hope for those striving to break into the charmed circle'

–RICHARD WATER, *Financial Times*

'*The Start-up of You* describes how to take the Silicon Valley approach to building a life: start with an idea, and work over your entire career to turn it into something remarkable. In the world today, I think that the startup approach to life is necessary. This book distils the key techniques needed to succeed.'

–JACK DORSEY, co-founder of Twitter, co-founder of Square

'Being an entrepreneur isn't really about starting a business. It's a way of looking at the world: seeing opportunity where others see obstacles, taking risks when others take refuge. Whatever career you're in or want to be in *The Start-up of You* holds lessons for success.'

–MICHAEL BLOOMBERG, founder of Bloomberg, L. P. and Mayor, New York City

The
START-UP of YOU

ADAPT TO THE FUTURE, INVEST IN YOURSELF,

AND TRANSFORM YOUR CAREER

Reid Hoffman and Ben Casnocha

BUSINESS
BOOKS

Published by Random House Business Books 2013

2 4 6 8 10 9 7 5 3 1

Copyright © Reid Hoffman and Ben Casnocha 2012

Reid Hoffman and Ben Casnocha have asserted their right under the Copyright,
Designs and Patents Act, 1988, to be identified as the authors of this work

First published in the United States in 2012 by Crown Business, an imprint of the
Crown Publishing Group, a division of Random House, Inc., New York

First published in Great Britain in 2012 by
Random House Business Books

Random House,
20 Vauxhall Bridge Road,
London SW1V 2SA

www.randomhouse.co.uk

Addresses for companies within The Random House Group Limited can be found at:
www.randomhouse.co.uk/offices.htm

The Random House Group Limited Reg. No. 954009

A CIP catalogue record for this book is
available from the British Library

ISBN 9781847940803

The Random House Group Limited supports The Forest Stewardship
Council (FSC®), the leading international forest certification organisation.
Our books carrying the FSC label are printed on FSC® certified paper. FSC is the
only forest certification scheme endorsed by the leading environmental organisations,
including Greenpeace. Our paper procurement policy can be found at:
www.randomhouse.co.uk/environment

Printed and bound by CPI Group (UK) Ltd, Croydon, CR0 4YY

To my mom and dad,
who have tried to teach me wisdom,
and to Michelle,
who tries to teach me compassion every day.
—RGH

•   •   •

To the Mac Doctor,
for inspiring me to Think Different.
—BTC

Contents

1

All Humans Are Entrepreneurs

All human beings are entrepreneurs. When we were in the caves, we were all self-employed . . . finding our food, feeding ourselves. That's where human history began. As civilization came, we suppressed it. We became "labor" because they stamped us, "You are labor." We forgot that we are entrepreneurs.

—*Muhammad Yunus,*
Nobel Peace Prize winner and microfinance pioneer

You were born an entrepreneur.

This doesn't mean you were born to start companies. In fact, most people shouldn't start companies. The long odds of success, combined with the constant emotional whiplash, makes starting a business the right path for only some people.

All humans are entrepreneurs not because they should start companies but because the will to create is encoded in human DNA, and creation is the essence of entrepreneurship. As Yunus says, our ancestors in the caves had to feed themselves; they had to invent rules of living. They were founders of their own lives. In the centuries since then we forgot that we are entrepreneurs. We've been acting like labor.

To adapt to the challenges of professional life today, we need to rediscover our entrepreneurial instincts and use them to forge new sorts of careers. Whether you're a lawyer or doctor or teacher or engineer or even a business owner, today you need to also think of yourself as an entrepreneur at the helm of at least one living, growing start-up venture: *your career.*

This book is not a job-hunting manual. You won't find tips and tricks on how to format your résumé or how to prepare for a job interview. What you will find are the start-up mind-sets and skill sets you need to adapt to the future. You'll find strategies that will help you expand the reach of your network, gain a competitive edge, and land better professional opportunities.

Your future success depends on understanding and deploying these entrepreneurial strategies. More broadly, society flourishes when people think entrepreneurially. More world problems will be solved—and solved faster—if people practice the values laid out in the pages ahead. This is a book about you, and it's also about improving the society around you. That starts with each individual.

THE NEW WORLD OF WORK

Centuries of immigrants risked everything to come to America with the conviction that if they worked hard, they would enjoy a better life than their parents had.[1] Since our country's birth, each generation of Americans has generally made more money, been better educated, and enjoyed a higher standard of living than the generation that came before it. An expectation of lockstep increases in prosperity became part of the American Dream.

For the last sixty or so years, the job market for educated workers worked like an escalator.[2] After graduating from college, you landed an entry-level job at the bottom of the escalator at an IBM or a GE or a Goldman Sachs. There you were groomed and mentored, receiving training and professional development from your employer. As you gained experience, you were whisked up the organizational hierarchy, clearing room for the ambitious young graduates who followed to fill the same entry-level positions. So long as you played nice and well, you moved steadily up the escalator, and each step brought with it more power, income, and job security. Eventually, around age sixty-five, you stepped off the escalator, allowing those middle-ranked employees to fill the same senior positions you just vacated. You, meanwhile, coasted into a comfortable retirement financed by a company pension and government-funded Social Security.

People didn't assume all of this necessarily happened automatically. But there was a sense that if you were basically competent, put forth a good effort, and weren't unlucky, the strong winds at your back would eventually shoot you to a good high level. For the most part this was a justified expectation.

But now that escalator is jammed at every level. Many young people, even the most highly educated, are stuck at the bottom, underemployed, or jobless, as Ronald Brownstein noted in the *Atlantic*.[3] At the same time, men and women in their sixties and seventies, with empty pensions and a government safety net that looks like Swiss cheese, are staying in or rejoining the workforce in record numbers.[4] At best, this keeps middle-aged workers stuck in promotionless limbo; at worst, it squeezes them out in order to make room for more-senior talent. Today, it's hard for the young to get on the escalator, it's hard for the middle-aged to ascend, and it's hard for anyone over sixty to get off. "Rather than advancing in smooth procession, everyone is stepping on everybody else," Brownstein says.

With the death of traditional career paths, so goes the kind of traditional professional development previous generations enjoyed. You can no longer count on employer-sponsored training to enhance your communication skills or expand your technical know-how. The expectation for even junior employees is that you can do the job you've been hired to do upon arrival or that you'll learn so quickly you'll be up to speed within weeks.[5] Whether you want to learn a new skill or simply be better at the job you were hired to do, it's now your job to train and invest in yourself. Companies don't want to invest in you, in part because you're not likely to commit years and years of your life to working there—you will have many different jobs in your lifetime. There used to be a long-term pact between employee and employer that guaranteed lifetime employment in exchange for lifelong loyalty; this pact has been replaced by a performance-based, short-term contract that's perpetually up for renewal by both sides. Professional loyalty now flows "horizontally" to and from your network rather than "vertically" to your boss, as Dan Pink has noted.

The undoing of these traditional career assumptions has to do with at least two interrelated macro forces: globalization and technology. These concepts may seem overhyped to you, but their long-term effects are actually underhyped. Technology automates jobs that used to require hard-earned knowledge and skills, including *well-paid*, white-collar jobs such as stockbrokers, paralegals, and radiologists.[6] Technology also creates new jobs, but this creation tends to lag the displacement, and the new jobs usually require different, higher-level skills than did the ones they replaced.[7] If technology doesn't eliminate or change the skills you need in many industries, it at least enables more people from around the world to compete for your job by allowing companies to offshore work more easily—knocking down your salary in the process. Trade and technology did not appear overnight and are not going away anytime soon. The labor market in which we all work has been permanently altered.

So forget what you thought you knew about the world of work. The rules have changed. "Ready, aim, fire" has been replaced by "Aim, fire, aim, fire, aim, fire." Searching for a job only when you're unemployed or unhappy at work has been replaced by the mandate to always be generating opportunities. Networking has been replaced by intelligent *network building*.

The gap is growing between those who know the new career rules and have the new skills of a global economy, and those who clutch to old ways of thinking and rely on commoditized skills. The question is, which are you?

WHY THE START-UP OF YOU

With change come new opportunities as well as challenges. What's required now is an entrepreneurial mind-set. Whether you work for a ten-person company, a giant multinational corporation, a not-for-profit, a government agency, or any type of organization in between—if you want to seize the new opportunities and meet the challenges of today's fractured career landscape, you need to think and act like you're running a start-up: your career.

Why the *start-up* of you? When you start a company, you make decisions in an information-poor, time-compressed, resource-constrained environment. There are no guarantees or safety nets, so you take on a certain amount of risk. The competition is changing; the market is changing. The life cycle of the company is fairly short. The conditions in which entrepreneurs start and grow companies are the conditions we *all* now live in when fashioning a career. You never know what's going to happen next. Information is limited. Resources are tight. Competition is fierce. The world is changing. And the amount of time you spend at any one job is shrinking. This means you need to be adapting all the time. And if you fail to adapt, no one—not your employer, not the government—is going to catch you when you fall.

Entrepreneurs deal with these uncertainties, changes, and constraints head-on. They take stock of their assets, aspirations, and the market realities to develop a competitive advantage. They craft flexible, iterative plans. They build a network of relationships throughout their industy that outlives their start-up. They aggressively seek and create breakout opportunities that involve focused risk, and actively manage that risk. They tap their network for the business intelligence to navigate tough challenges. And, they do these things from the moment they hatch that nascent idea to every day after that—even as the companies go from being run out of a garage to occupying floors of office space. *To succeed professionally in today's world, you need to adopt these same entrepreneurial strategies.*

They are valuable no matter your career stage. They are urgent whether you're just out of college, a decade into the workforce and angling for that next big move, or launching a brand-new career later in life. Companies act small to retain an innovative edge no matter how large they grow. Steve Jobs called Apple the "biggest start-up on the planet." In the same way, you need to stay young and agile; you need to forever be a *start-up*.

WHY US?

I (Reid) cofounded LinkedIn in 2003 with the mission of connecting the world's professionals to make them more productive and successful. More than 100 million members (at the time of the LinkedIn IPO in May 2011) and nine years later, I've learned a tremendous amount about how professionals in every industry manage their careers: how they connect with trusted business contacts, find jobs, share information, and present their online identities. For example, from LinkedIn's massive professional engagement, my colleagues and I have gleaned insights about the most-sought-after skills, industry trends, and the career paths that lead to opportunities. I've gleaned insight about which approaches succeed and which fail; which tactics work and which fall flat. Along the way, I began to notice something utterly fascinating that related to my other passion: investing.

As executive chairman, LinkedIn is my primary day job, but I also invest in other start-ups. As an angel investor and now as partner at Greylock, I've invested in more than one hundred companies. This has given me an opportunity to help awesome entrepreneurs scale their businesses: be it brainstorming with Mark Pincus at Zynga on social gaming strategy, thinking through the future of the mobile Internet with Kevin Rose at Digg and Milk (his mobile apps firm), or collaborating with Matt Flannery to bring Kiva's microloan model to all the world's poor. Through these diverse experiences, I've developed an eye for the patterns of success and the patterns of failure in entrepreneurship.

Wearing these two hats—helping LinkedIn enable more economic opportunity for our members as well as helping my other portfolio companies grow—led me to a revelation: The business strategies employed by highly successful *start-ups* and the career strategies employed by highly successful *individuals* are strikingly similar. Ever since, I've been distilling into strategic frameworks all that I've learned from twenty fortunate years in Silicon Valley and applying them to the idea that every individual is a small business. I think about my own career in exactly this way: as a start-up.

When I first met Ben, he was at a career juncture: he was deciding whether to do more tech entrepreneurship (he had already started a couple of companies), more writing (he had written a book about entrepreneurship), more international travel (he had traveled abroad extensively), or some combination of all of them. Then in his early twenties, he was grappling with questions like: How far in the future should he plan? What kinds of career risks are advisable? How does someone experiment broadly *and* build specialized expertise? Then he said something that intrigued me. He told me that even if his next move wasn't to start a new company, he still was going to approach all of these critical career questions as an entrepreneur would.

In the months leading up to our first meeting, Ben visited dozens of countries and met thousands of students, entrepreneurs, journalists, and businesspeople—from community college students in middle America to small-business owners in rural Indonesia to government leaders in Colombia. In these far-flung places he spoke about his own experiences and simultaneously observed and learned about the aspirations and attitudes of the talented local people. The remarkable thing he noticed was that entrepreneurship—in the broad sense of the word—was everywhere: thousands of miles from Silicon Valley, in the hearts and minds of people not necessarily starting companies. While they may not have considered themselves entrepreneurs, their approach to life seemed every bit the Silicon Valley way: they were self-reliant in spirit, resourceful, ambitious, adaptive, and networked with one another. From these experiences he arrived separately at the same conclusion that I did: entrepreneurship is a *life* idea, not a strictly business one; a *global* idea, not a strictly American one. (Which I also experienced by serving on the board of the global entrepreneurship organization Endeavor.) And, as the two decades between us attest, it's also a *lifelong* idea, not a generational one.

WHY THE URGENCY?

Before we look forward at how entrepreneurship as a life idea can transform your career, we first need to understand what's at stake. There's no better way to demonstrate the perils of failing to adapt the start-up of you mind-set than by looking back at an industry that *once* embodied the best of entrepreneurship: Detroit.

In the middle of the twentieth century, Detroit flourished into a dynamic capital of the world thanks to three local start-ups: Ford Motor Company, General Motors, and Chrysler. At the time, these automakers were as innovative as they come. Ford figured out a way to mass-produce cars and trucks on an assembly line, a technique that changed manufacturing forever. GM and its legendary chairman Alfred Sloan developed a system of management and organization that was imitated by hundreds of other corporations. They were also visionaries. They boldly believed (when few did) that cars would be ubiquitous in a country that celebrated the idea of an open frontier. Alfred Sloan promised "a car for every purse and purpose." Henry Ford said he would build a car "so low in price that no man making a good salary will be unable to own one."

Like the best entrepreneurs, they did more than just dream. They went out and created the future they had imagined. Collectively, in the latter half of the twentieth century, American carmakers produced hundreds of millions of innovative, stylish vehicles, and sold them to customers in every part of the world. In 1955 GM became the first corporation in history to earn a billion dollars of revenue.[8] By the end of that decade, GM was a juggernaut so powerful that the Justice Department considered breaking it up.

A job at these companies perfectly embodied the old career escalator. There was unbeatable job security—almost no one got fired from car companies. If you lacked the necessary skills, your employer would train you. General Motors even ran its own undergraduate university, a mix of classroom study and factory work. Graduating from its institute virtually guaranteed lifelong employment and its accompanying benefits. As you accumulated years on the job, you ascended in job rank.

During the boom years of the auto industry, the city of Detroit prospered. It was the land of dreams, riches, and next-generation technology. "This was Silicon Valley, man," local newspaper columnist Tom Walsh told us, reflecting on Detroit's golden age. Entrepreneurs were taking home colossal fortunes, and a million new people flooded into Detroit wanting a piece of it—an influx that made Detroit the fourth-most-populous city in the country.[9] Wages were high; the city's median income was the highest in America. Home ownership soared. Aside from being a great place to make a living, Detroit boasted a diversity, energy, culture, and progressive spirit that rivaled Chicago and New York. It was the first city to assign individual telephone numbers, pave a mile of concrete road, and develop an urban freeway.

In the 1940s, '50s, and '60s, Detroit was a crown jewel of America. "The word *Detroit* is a synonym throughout the world for the industrial greatness of America," boomed President Harry Truman at the time.[10] It was a key part of the "arsenal of democracy," so symbolic of American exceptionalism that visitors from around the world flocked there to get a glimpse of entrepreneurship and innovation at its very best.

Then Detroit's automakers lost their entrepreneurial spirit. The entrepreneurs became labor. And like the *Titanic* colliding with the tip of a giant iceberg, Detroit started to sink slowly to the bottom.

Sixty to Zero

"Year after year, decade after decade, we have seen problems papered over and tough choices kicked down the road, even as foreign competitors outpaced us. Well, we have reached the end of that road," said President Barack Obama in 2009, at a press conference announcing that the federal government was loaning $77 billion to GM and Chrysler (and granting access to a line of credit to Ford) to prop up the companies as they filed for Chapter 11 bankruptcy.[11] For older Americans who grew up enchanted by the grandeur of Detroit, President

Obama's announcement neatly summed up three decades of decay and disillusionment.

What happened? Many things. But the overriding problem was this: The auto industry got too comfortable. As Intel cofounder Andy Grove once famously proclaimed, "Only the paranoid survive." Success, he meant, is fragile—and perfection, fleeting. The moment you begin to take success for granted is the moment a competitor lunges for your jugular. Auto industry executives, to say the least, were not paranoid.

Instead of listening to a customer base that wanted smaller, more fuel-efficient cars, the auto executives built bigger and bigger. Instead of taking seriously new competition from Japan, they staunchly insisted (both to themselves and to their customers) that MADE IN THE USA automatically meant "best in the world." Instead of trying to learn from their competitors' new methods of "lean manufacturing," they clung stubbornly to their decades-old practices. Instead of rewarding the best people in the organization and firing the worst, they promoted on the basis of longevity and nepotism. Instead of moving quickly to keep up with the changing market, executives willingly embraced "death by committee." Ross Perot once quipped that if a man saw a snake on the factory floor at GM, they'd form a committee to analyze whether they should kill it.

Easy success had transformed the American auto companies into risk-averse, nonmeritocratic, bloated bureaucracies. When the competition heated up and customer needs changed, the company executives and the autoworker employee unions did not adapt. Instead, they did more of the same.

Detroit did not burst overnight. It saw a gradual deflation. In fact, that was part of the problem. Because companies were still generating billions of dollars of revenue for years during their decline, it was easy for management to get complacent, to ignore the problems that were piling up. No one stress-tested the organization, or tried to identify and fix long-term weaknesses. This made the day of reckoning painful. By the time the red alarm started ringing—that is, when GM lost $82 *billion* in the three and a half years leading up to the federal bailout—it was too late.

The auto industry's collapse has left the Motor City in dire straits. "The great thing about living in America's most abandoned city," deadpanned Walsh, the local columnist, "is that there is never any traffic at any hour." *Abandoned* is certainly the word that comes to mind if you walk the streets just outside of the main downtown drag in Detroit. You can go blocks without seeing anybody. Empty houses languish. Some are professionally boarded up, with CONDEMNED signs tacked to the front door; others have only black tarp stapled within empty window frames. Many buildings bear an eerie resemblance to crumbling gingerbread houses. About a third of the city—an area the size of San Francisco—is deserted.

For those who remain, life is grim. Detroit is the second-most-dangerous city in the United States (behind Flint, Michigan). Half of its children live in poverty. It leads the country in unemployment—estimates run anywhere from 15 to 50 percent. The school system is a travesty: eight out of ten eighth-graders are unable to do basic math.[12] Most local politicians are variously corrupt and inept. Unbelievably, there is not one produce-carrying grocery chain in the whole city.

Detroit was once the symbol of progress, of what is good and possible. The auto industry was once the symbol of entrepreneurship. Now Detroit is the symbol of despair.

Detroits Are Everywhere

The story of Detroit isn't simple. There are other complicating factors we haven't mentioned in our brief sketch, and there are early indicators that things may be improving. Nor is the Detroit story unique. We hold the auto industry up as an example not because it's exceptional, but because it *isn't*. Recent history teems with industries and companies that have experienced similarly precipitous declines. Once-great companies are falling both more frequently and more quickly than in times past. In the 1920s and '30s firms stayed in the S&P 500 for an average of sixty-five years. By the late 1990s the average tenure was just ten years. John Seely Brown and John Hagel, of Deloitte, report that the *topple rate*—the rate at which big companies lose their leadership positions—has more than doubled over the past forty years. Today more than ever, " 'winners' have increasingly precarious positions."[13]

Why are so many winners ending up like Detroit? Each case is different, but underlying causes tend to include the hubris that comes from success, the failure to recognize and match competition, an unwillingness to exploit opportunities that contain risk, and an inability to adapt to relentless change. The forces of competition and change that brought down Detroit are global and local. They threaten every business, every industry, every city. And more important, *they also threaten every individual, every career.*

This is not a book about the economic history of Detroit. So why is Detroit important? Because no matter what city you live in, no matter what business or industry you work for, no matter what kind of work you do—*when it comes to your career, right now, you may be heading down the same path as Detroit.* The forces of change that toppled the once great city and industry risk toppling all of our careers—no matter how secure they may seem at the moment.

Fortunately, there is another path—both metaphorically and physically thousands of miles away from Detroit. Silicon Valley has become the twenty-first-century model for entrepreneurship and progress and has had multiple generations of entrepreneurial companies over the decades: from Hewlett Packard's founding in 1939 to Intel, Apple, Adobe, Genentech, AMD, Intuit, Oracle, Electronic Arts, Pixar, and Cisco, and then to Google, eBay, Yahoo, Seagate, and Salesforce, and then more recently to PayPal, Facebook, YouTube, Craigslist, Twitter, and LinkedIn.

In each passing decade, Silicon Valley has kept and intensified its entrepreneurial mojo, with dozens of companies creating the future and adapting to the evolution of the global market. These companies provide not only a new model for corporate innovation, but also the entrepreneur mind-set needed to succeed in individual careers.

What do these companies have in common? The principles of Silicon Valley are the principles in this book. Take intelligent and bold risks to accomplish something great. Build a network of alliances to help you with intelligence, resources, and collective action. Pivot to a breakout opportunity.

You can think like a start-up, whoever you are and whatever you do. Anyone can apply this entrepreneurial skill set to his or her career. This is a book about how to do just that. It's about keeping Detroit from happening *to* you and making the Silicon Valley way work *for* you.

THE PATH TO THE FUTURE

In 1997 Reed Hastings, a software entrepreneur living in the hills of Silicon Valley, was faced with a problem. He had rented *Apollo 13* from a video store, returned it days late, and was dealt a late fee so nasty that he was too embarrassed to tell his wife what had happened. His entrepreneurial instinct kicked in: What if you could rent a movie and never face the risk of a late fee? So he began researching the industry and learned that the new DVD technology was light and cheap to ship.[14] He realized that the shift toward e-commerce, in concert with the DVD revolution, could be a huge opportunity. So that year he launched a business that combined e-commerce with old-fashioned postal mail: customers would select their movie on a website, receive a DVD of the movie in the mail, and then mail it back whenever they were finished. It was a compelling idea, but Reed knew from his years in the technology industry that it would inevitably evolve. He avoided calling his business DVDs-by-Mail (or some other name that was specific to the business's current iteration) and instead came up with a more expansive company name: Netflix.

Netflix wasn't instantly successful. Originally, customers paid for each DVD they rented, like at Blockbuster, the industry gorilla that operated thousands of video rental stores worldwide.[15] It didn't catch on. So Reed began offering monthly subscription plans that allowed unlimited rentals. Yet customers still complained that it took too long from the time they selected a flick online to when it arrived in the mail. In 1999 he set up a meeting at Blockbuster's headquarters in part to discuss possibly partnering on local distribution and faster fulfillment. Blockbuster was not impressed. "They just about laughed us out of their office," Reed recalls.[16]

Reed and his team kept at it. They perfected their distribution center network so that more than 80 percent of customers received overnight delivery of movies.[17] They developed an innovative recommendation engine that prompted users with movies they might like based on past purchases. By 2005 Netflix had a subscriber base four million strong, had fended off competition from imitations like Walmart's online movie-by-mail effort, and became the king of online movie rentals. In 2010 Netflix made a profit of more than $160 million. Blockbuster, in comparison, failed to adapt to the Internet era. That year it filed for bankruptcy.[18]

Netflix is not resting. In fact, in 2010 and 2011 the company shifted focus from its still profitable DVDs-by-mail business and jumped to the next curve: instant online streaming of movies and TV shows to computers, smart-phones, and tablet devices. It's something they'd wanted to do for years, and wide-scale broadband adoption now allows it. The majority of their customers now watch TV shows and movies via streaming rather than by DVD, and, at the time of writing, Netflix accounts for more than 30 percent of all Internet traffic during the week. Soon, online streaming may well feature significant Netflix original programming, or incorporate some new technology not yet invented. Nonetheless, their ongoing success is not assured. There are always new challenges.

"Most of the time, change in the world overtakes you," Reed says. When a Hollywood executive once asked him during an on-stage interview whether he makes five-year strategic plans or three-year strategic plans, Reed said he does neither: three years is an eternity in Silicon Valley, and they can't plan that far in advance. Instead, Netflix stays nimble and iterates, always in the test phase. We call this mind-set "permanent beta."

The Start-up of You Mind-set: Permanent Beta

Technology companies sometimes keep the beta test phase label on software for a time after the official launch to stress that the product is not finished so much as ready for the next batch of improvements. Gmail, for example, launched in 2004 but only left official beta in 2009, after millions of people were already using it. Jeff Bezos, founder/CEO of

Amazon, concludes every annual letter to shareholders by reminding readers, as he did in his first annual letter in 1997, that "it's still Day 1" of the Internet and of Amazon.com: "Though we are optimistic, we must remain vigilant and maintain a sense of urgency."[19] In other words, Amazon is never finished: it's always Day 1. For entrepreneurs, *finished* is an F-word. They know that great companies are always evolving.

Finished ought to be an F-word for all of us. *We are all works in progress.* Each day presents an opportunity to learn more, do more, be more, grow more in our lives and careers. Keeping your career in permanent beta forces you to acknowledge that you have bugs, that there's new development to do on yourself, that you will need to adapt and evolve. But it's still a mind-set brimming with optimism because it celebrates the fact that you have the power to improve yourself and, as important, improve the world around you.

Andy Hargadon, head of the entrepreneurship center at the University of California–Davis, says that for many people "twenty years of experience" is really one year of experience repeated twenty times.[20] If you're in permanent beta in your career, twenty years of experience actually is twenty years of experience because each year will be marked by new, enriching challenges and opportunities. Permanent beta is essentially a lifelong commitment to continuous personal growth.

Get busy livin', or get busy dyin'. If you're not growing, you're contracting. If you're not moving forward, you're moving backward.

The Start-up of You Skill Set

The permanent beta mind-set alone won't transform your career. There are real skills involved in becoming the entrepreneur of your own life. In the following chapters, we'll introduce how to:

- Develop your **competitive advantage** in the market by combining three puzzle pieces: your **assets**, your **aspirations**, and the **market realities**. (Chapter 2)
- Use **ABZ Planning** to formulate a Plan A based on your competitive advantages, and then iterate and **adapt** that plan based on feedback and lessons learned. (Chapter 3)
- Build real, lasting **relationships** and deploy these relationships into a powerful **professional network**. (Chapter 4)
- Find and create **opportunities** for yourself by tapping **networks**, being **resourceful**, and staying in **motion**. (Chapter 5)
- Accurately appraise and take on **intelligent risk** as you pursue professional opportunities. (Chapter 6)
- Tap **network intelligence** from the people you know for the insight that allows you to find better opportunities and make better career decisions. (Chapter 7)

At the end of each chapter, we include specific action items on how to invest in yourself.

These skills do not cover all things related to work and careers. Nor is this book an analysis of all ideas related to entrepreneurship. Instead, we draw on the entrepreneurial strategies that can help you achieve the following two goals.

First, we will show how to survive in times of change and uncertainty to avoid the fate of Detroit. We'll show you how to get healthy stability in your career by *adapting*. Adaptability creates stability.

Second, we aim to equip you with the strategies that help you break out from the pack and flourish as a globally competitive professional. Whether you want to move up in a corporation, start your own small business, or transition into an entirely new industry—whatever your ambitions for a successful career, we'll show you how you can achieve them by thinking and acting like an entrepreneur. These entrepreneurial career strategies aren't a magic bullet. But they will help you move up that jammed escalator and not only survive, but thrive, in today's fractured world of work.

Let's get going. You have a start-up to run.

Develop a Competitive Advantage

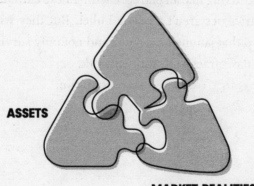

ASPIRATIONS

ASSETS

MARKET REALITIES

A billboard that sat along the 101 Highway in the Bay Area in 2009 put it bluntly: "1,000,000 people overseas can do your job. What makes you so special?"[1] While one million might be an exaggeration, what's not an exaggeration is that lots of other people *can* and *want* to have your dream job. For anything desirable, there's competition: a ticket to a championship game, the arm of an attractive man or woman, admission to a good college, and every solid professional opportunity.

Being better than the competition is basic to an entrepreneur's survival. In every sector multiple companies compete over a single customer's dollar. The world is loud and messy; customers don't have time to parse minute differences. If a company's product isn't massively different from a competitor's—as Do Something CEO Nancy Lublin says, unless it's first, only, faster, better, or cheaper—it's not going to command anyone's attention. Good entrepreneurs build and brand products that are differentiated from the competition. They are able to finish the sentence, "Our customers buy from us and not that other company because . . ."

Zappos.com, the online shoe retailer founded in 1999, has a clear answer to that question: insanely good customer service. While other online shoe stores like shoebuy and on-lineshoes.com offered 30-day return windows, Zappos made a name for itself by being the first to offer a 365-day return policy on everything they sold. While retailers like L.L. Bean and J.Crew expected customers to pick up the shipping costs each time they returned something from an online order, Zappos offered free shipping on all returns, no questions asked. And even when giants like The Gap mimicked the free shipping and free returns offer in their online shoe store, they buried a customer service phone number in small print at the bottom of the page. Zappos' 1-800 number, on the other hand, is displayed "proudly," in CEO Tony Hsieh's words, on every single page of its website. Moreover, local employees working at corporate headquarters in Nevada answer every call. There are no scripts and no time limits on such calls—virtually unheard of in an age of quota-driven, out-sourced customer service centers. Zappos massively differentiated itself from its competition by building a culture that is customer-centric in every way imaginable. This is what has made Zappos a trusted destination for millions of loyal online shoppers (and it's also why it was acquired by Amazon for close to a billion dollars).

Yes, you are different from an online shoe store. But you are selling your brainpower, your skills, your energy. And you are doing so in the face of massive competition. Possible employers, partners, investors, and other people with power choose between you and someone who looks like you. When a desirable opportunity arises, many people with similar job titles and educational backgrounds will be considered. When sifting through applications for almost any job, employers and hiring managers are quickly overcome by the sameness.[2] It's a blur.

If you want to chart a course that differentiates you from other professionals in the marketplace, the first step is being able to complete the sentence, "A company hires me over other professionals because . . ." How are you first, only, faster, better, or cheaper than other people who want to do what you're doing in the world? What are you offering that's hard to come by? What are you offering that's both rare and valuable?

You don't need to be better or faster or cheaper than *everyone*. Companies, after all, don't compete in every product category or offer every conceivable service. Zappos focuses on mainstream shoes and clothes. If it tried to offer over-the-top customer service on a range of high-end luxury products, it couldn't be the place for quality shoes delivered with terrific service, because its focus would be diluted and its differentiation eroded. In life, there are multiple gold medals. If you try to be the best at everything and better than everyone (that is, if you believe success means ascending one global, mega leaderboard), you'll be the best at nothing and better than no one. Instead, compete in local contests—local not just in terms of geography but also in terms of industry segment and skill set. In other words, don't try to be the greatest marketing executive in the world; try to be the greatest marketing executive of small-to-midsize companies that compete in the health-care industry. Don't just try to be the highest-paid hospitality operations person in the world; try to be a top-notch hospitality operations person in a way that's aligned with your values so that you can sustain your work over the long run. What we explain in this chapter is how to determine the local niche in which *you* can develop a competitive advantage.

Competitive advantage underpins all career strategy. It helps answer the classic question, "What should I be doing with my life?" It helps you decide which opportunities to pursue. It guides you in how you should be investing in yourself. Because all of these things change, assessing and evaluating your competitive advantage is a lifelong process, not something you do once. And it's done by understanding three dynamic puzzle pieces that fit together in different ways at different times.

THREE PUZZLE PIECES INFORM YOUR DIRECTION AND COMPETITIVE ADVANTAGE

Your competitive advantage is formed by the interplay of three different, ever-changing forces: your assets, your aspirations/values, and the market realities, i.e., the supply and demand for what you offer the marketplace relative to the competition. The best direction has you pursuing worthy aspirations, using your assets, while navigating the market realities. We're not expecting you to already have a clear understanding of each of these pieces. As we show in the next chapter, the best way to learn about these things is by *doing*. But we want to introduce the concepts so you can begin to understand how they work, and how they inform the career decisions we'll talk about in the rest of the book.

Your Assets

Assets are what you have right now. Before dreaming about the future or making plans, you need to articulate what you already have going for you—as entrepreneurs do. The most brilliant business idea is often the one that builds on the founders' existing assets in the most brilliant way. There are reasons Larry Page and Sergey Brin started Google and Donald Trump started a real estate firm. Page and Brin were in a computer science doctoral program. Trump's father was a wealthy real estate developer, and he had apprenticed in his father's firm for five years. Their business goals emerged from their strengths, interests, and network of contacts.

You have two types of career assets to keep track of: soft and hard. Soft assets are things you can't trade directly for money. They're the intangible contributors to career success: the knowledge and information in your brain; professional connections and the trust you've built up with them; skills you've mastered; your reputation and personal brand; your strengths (things that come easily to you).

Hard assets are what you'd typically list on a balance sheet: the cash in your wallet; the stocks you own; physical possessions like your desk and laptop. These matter because when you have an economic cushion, you can more aggressively make moves that entail downside financial risk. For example, you could take six months off to learn the Ruby programming language with no pay—i.e., pick up a new skill. Or you could shift to a lower-paying but more stimulating job opportunity.

During a career transition, someone who can go six to twelve months without earning money has different options—indeed, a significant advantage—over someone who can't go more than a month or two without a paycheck.

Soft assets are more difficult to tally than cash in a bank account, but assuming your basic economic needs are taken care of, soft assets are ultimately more important. Dominating a professional project at work has little to do with how much dough you've socked away in a savings account; what matters are skills, connections, experiences. Because soft assets may be abstract, there's a tendency for people to underestimate them when pondering career strategy. People list impressive-sounding-yet-vague statements like "I have two years of experience working at a marketing firm . . ." instead of specifying, explicitly and clearly, what they are able to do *because* of those two years of experience. One of the best ways to remember how rich you are in intangible wealth—that is, the value of your soft assets—is to go to a networking event and ask people about their professional problems or needs. You'll be surprised how many times you have a helpful idea, know somebody relevant, or think to yourself, "I could solve that pretty easily." Often it's when you come in contact with challenges *other* people find hard but *you* find easy that you know you're in possession of a valuable soft asset.[3]

Usually, however, single assets in isolation don't have much value. A competitive edge emerges when you combine different skills, experiences, and connections. For example, Joi Ito, a friend and head of the MIT Media Lab, was born in Japan but raised in Michigan. In his mid-twenties he moved back to

Japan and set up one of the first commercial Internet service providers there. He also kept developing connections in the United States, investing in Silicon Valley start-ups like Flickr and Twitter, establishing the Japanese subsidiary for the early American blogging company Six Apart, and more recently helping to establish LinkedIn Japan. Is Joi the only person with start-up experience who does angel investing in the Valley? No. Is he the only person with roots in both the United States and Japan? No. But combining these transpacific, bilingual, tech-industry assets gives him a competitive advantage over other investors and entrepreneurs.

Your asset mix is not fixed. You can strengthen it by investing in yourself—that's what this book is about. So if you think you lack certain assets that would make you more competitive, don't use it as an excuse. Start developing them. In the meantime, see how you can turn a weakness into a strength. For example, you may not see inexperience as an asset to highlight, but the flip side of inexperience tends to be energy, enthusiasm, and a willingness to work and hustle in order to learn.

Your Aspirations and Values

Aspirations and values are the second consideration. Aspirations include your deepest wishes, ideas, goals, and vision of the future, regardless of the state of the external world or your existing asset mix. This piece of the puzzle includes your core values, or what's important to you in life, be it knowledge, autonomy, money, integrity, power, and so on. You may not be able to achieve all your aspirations or build a life that incorporates all your values. And they will certainly change over time. But you should at least orient yourself in the direction of a pole star, even if it changes.

Jack Dorsey is cofounder and executive chairman of Twitter and cofounder and CEO of Square, a mobile credit card payments start-up. He's known in Silicon Valley as a product visionary who prizes design and who takes inspiration from sources as varied as Steve Jobs and the Golden Gate Bridge. Both his companies have grown to towering heights (and multibillion-dollar valuations) while keeping Jack's values and priorities intact. Twitter is still minimalistic and clean; the Square device is still elegant. His aspiration to make complex things simple and his value of design are part of the reason his companies have been so successful: they clarify product priorities, ensure a consistent customer experience, and make it easier to recruit employees who are attracted to similar ideas. For a start-up, a compelling vision that acts as a pole star is a meaningful piece of a company's competitive advantage. Google's clarity of purpose to "organize the world's information," for example, has drawn some of the brightest engineering minds while at the same time been broad enough to allow adaptation and reinvention.

Aspirations and values are both important pieces of your career competitive advantage quite simply because when you're doing work you care about, you are able to work harder and better. The person passionate about what he or she is doing will outwork and outlast the guy motivated solely by making money. It can be easy to forget this when heading the start-up of you. In an effort to scrappily improve on who you are *today*, you can lose track of who you *aspire* to be in the future. For example, if you're currently an analyst at Morgan Stanley, the savviest way to leverage your existing assets may be to angle for a promotion within the firm. If the banking industry is in a slump, the savviest way to attend to the market realities may be to develop skills in a different but related industry, like accounting. But would these moves reflect what you really care about?

That said, and contrary to what many bestselling authors and motivational gurus would have you believe, there is not a "true self" deep within that you can uncover via introspection and that will point you in the right direction.[4] Yes, your aspirations shape what you do. But your aspirations are themselves shaped by your actions and experiences. You remake yourself as you grow and as the world changes. Your identity doesn't get found. It *emerges*.

Accept the uncertainty, especially early on. Ben, for example, knows he values intellectual stimulation and trying to change real people's lives through entrepreneurship and writing—though in what specific ways, he's still figuring out. Entrepreneur and writer Chris Yeh says his career mission is to "help interesting people do interesting things." That may sound airy, but it has real meaning: *interesting* reinforces the kind of stimulation he's looking for, and *do* means "do," not "think about." Later in your career, you may have more specific, thought-out aspirations. These are not unlike a start-up's mission statement. My pole star is to design and build human ecosystems using entrepreneurship, technology, and finance.

I build networks of people using entrepreneurship, finance, and technology as enablers. Whatever your values and aspirations, know that they will evolve over time.

The Market Realities

The realities of the world you live in is the final piece of the puzzle. Smart entrepreneurs know a product won't make money if customers don't want or need it, regardless of how slick its form and function (think of the Segway). Likewise, your skills, experiences, and other soft assets—no matter how special you think they are—won't give you an edge unless they meet the needs of a paying market. If Joi were bilingual in an obscure African dialect as opposed to the language of the world's third-largest economy (Japan), it wouldn't contribute to a compelling advantage for working with technology companies. And keep in mind that the "market" is not an abstract thing. It consists of the people who make decisions that affect you and whose needs you must serve: your boss, your coworkers, your clients, your direct reports, and others. How badly do they need what you have to offer, and if they need it, do you offer value that's better than the competition?

It's often said that entrepreneurs are dreamers. True. But good entrepreneurs are also firmly grounded in what's available and possible right now. Specifically, entrepreneurs spend vast amounts of energy trying to figure out what customers will pay for. Because ultimately, the success of all businesses depends on customers willing to sign on the line that is dotted. In turn, the success of all professionals—the start-up of you—depends on employers and clients and partners choosing to buy your time.

In 1985, when Howard Schultz (current CEO of Starbucks) was preparing to launch coffee bars in America modeled after those already in Italy, he and his partners didn't just launch the stores on a whim. They first did everything in their power to understand the dynamics of the market they were entering. They visited five hundred espresso bars in Milan and Verona to learn as much as they possibly could. How did the Italians design their cafés? What were the local coffee-drinking habits? How did the baristas serve coffee? What did the menus look like? They scribbled observations in notebooks. They videotaped the stores in action.[5] This kind of market research is not a one-time thing entrepreneurs do when a start-up first launches, either. David Neeleman founded his own airline, JetBlue Airways, and served as CEO for the first seven years. During that time he flew his own airline at least once a week, worked the cabin, and blogged about his experience: "Each week I fly on JetBlue flights and talk to customers so I can find out how we can improve our airline," he wrote.[6]

Schultz and Neeleman had tremendous vision when they founded their start-ups. Yet from day one they focused on the needs of their customers and stakeholders. For all their smarts and vision, they knew well what VC and friend Marc

Andreessen likes to say: Markets that don't exist don't care how smart you are. Similarly, it doesn't matter how hard you've worked or how passionate you are about an aspiration: If someone won't pay you for your services in the career marketplace, it's going to be a very hard slog. You aren't entitled to anything.

Studying the market realities doesn't have to be a limiting, negative exercise. There are always industries, places, people, and companies with momentum. Put yourself in a position to ride these waves. The Chinese economy, the politician Cory Booker, environmentally friendly consumer products: each is a big wave. Being in a position to ride them—making the market realities work for you as opposed to against you—is key to achieving breakout professional success.

FIT THE PIECES TOGETHER

A good career plan accounts for the interplay of the three pieces—your assets, aspirations, and the market realities. The pieces need to fit together. Developing a key skill, for example, doesn't automatically give you a competitive edge. Just because you're good at something (assets) that you're really passionate about (aspirations) doesn't necessarily mean someone will pay you to do it (market realities). After all, what if someone else can do the same thing for lower pay or do it more reliably? Or what if there's no demand for the skill to begin with? Not much of a competitive advantage. Following your passions also doesn't automatically lead to career flourishing.

What if you're passionate but not competent, relative to others? Finally, being a slave to market realities isn't sustainable. A shortage of nurses in hospitals—meaning there's demand for credentialed nurses—doesn't mean *you* should get on the nursing track. No matter what the demand, you're not going to be most competitive unless your own passions and strengths are in play.

So evaluate each piece of the puzzle in the context of the others. And do so regularly: the pieces of the puzzle change in shape and size over time. The way they fit together shifts over time. Building a competitive advantage in the marketplace involves combining the three pieces at every career juncture.

For a long time, business was not among my assets, aspirations, or the reality that I perceived around me. I attended the progressive Putney School in Vermont for high school, where I farmed maple syrup, drove oxen, and debated practical topics like epistemology (the nature of knowledge) with my teachers. In college and graduate school, I studied cognitive science, philosophy, and politics. I formed a conviction that I wanted to try to change the world for the better. Initially, my plan was to be an academic and public intellectual. At the time, I got bored easily (still do), which made me distractible and not great at making the trains run on time. Academia seemed like an environment that would keep me perpetually stimulated as I would think and write on the value of compassion, self-development, and the pursuit of wisdom. I would hopefully inspire others to implement these ideas to form a nobler society.

But graduate school, while stimulating, turned out to be

grounded in a culture and incentive scheme that promoted hyperspecialization; I discovered that academics end up writing for a scholarly elite of typically about fifty people. It turned out there was not much support for academics who would attempt to spread ideas to the masses. So my aspiration to have a broad impact on potentially millions of people clashed with the market realities of academia.

I adapted my career orientation. My new aim was to try to promote the workings of a good society via entrepreneurship and technology, the details of which we discuss in the next chapter. When I adapted and first thought about going into industry, I conducted informal informational interviews with friends from college who worked at companies like NeXT. I called them to figure out which skills I'd have to learn (e.g., writing product requirement documents) and the connections I'd have to build (e.g., working relationships with engineers). During my first technology job at Apple, one of the things I had to learn was Adobe Photoshop, for creating product mock-ups. Locking myself in a room for a weekend and becoming a Photoshop ninja was not an endeavor I thought was important while studying philosophy. However, being able to use Photoshop was necessary to pursue a product development career and therefore I learned it in order to advance in the industry. Trade-offs are inevitable when you're balancing different considerations such as the market realities of employment and your own natural interests.

Even as I have developed a career in the technology industry I have not relinquished my original aspirations. In fact, the issues of personal identity and community incentives that

I researched in academia are relevant to my current entrepreneurial passion for the social Web, online networks, and marketplaces. My longstanding interests in these themes have helped me develop industry skills and differentiation around the creation of massive Internet platforms.

Recently, I made a career move to start doing venture investing at Greylock. Again, I built on my assets and pursued my aspirations in the local environment in which I found myself. My significant operating experience at scale differentiates me from other VCs with finance backgrounds or limited operational backgrounds. This gives me a meaningful advantage in how I can partner with entrepreneurs and help them succeed. And since I can work with entrepreneurs whose companies build and define massive human ecosystems, I can help improve society at large scale, which meets my aspirations as a public intellectual. The three pieces fit.

All Advantages Are Local: Pick a Hill That Has Less Competition

The most obvious way to improve your competitive advantage is to strengthen and diversify your asset mix—for example, learn new skills. That's certainly smart. But it's equally effective to place yourself in a market niche where your existing assets shine brighter than the competition's. For example, top American college basketball players who aren't good enough to play professionally Stateside frequently play in European leagues. Instead of changing their skills, they change their local environment. They know they have a competitive advantage in a market with lower-quality competition.

Especially in the start-up world, competition—or lack thereof—makes a big difference. LinkedIn, from the outset, struck a different path from its competitors. In 2003, when LinkedIn started, its competitors were largely enterprise focused. Enterprise networks tied a person's profile and identity to a specific company and employer. Instead, LinkedIn placed the individual professional at the center of the system. LinkedIn's founding belief was that all individuals should own and manage their identities. They should be able to connect with people from other companies to work more effectively in their current jobs and find strong opportunities when they change jobs. LinkedIn had the right philosophy. The large social networks like Friendster, MySpace, and now Facebook have massive popularity, but none truly serves the needs of professionals. LinkedIn continues to invest in features that appeal to professionals and skips features like photo sharing or games that don't contribute to its competitive advantage. LinkedIn competes in the event where it can win the gold medal; it leads the space it has defined.

You can carve out a similar professional niche in the job market by making choices that make you different from the smart people around you. Matt Cohler, now a partner at Benchmark Capital, spent six years in his late twenties and early thirties being a lieutenant to CEOs at LinkedIn (me) and Facebook (Mark Zuckerberg). Most supertalented people want to be the front man; few play the consigliere role well. In other words, there's less competition and significant opportunity to be an all-star right-hand man. Matt excelled at this role, building a portfolio of accomplishments and relationships along the way. This professional differentiation in the market set him up to achieve a long-standing goal, which was to become a partner at a top-tier VC firm.

* * *

The three puzzle pieces become actionable when part of a good plan. In the next chapter we'll explore themes of planning, adapting, and *doing*.

INVEST IN YOURSELF

In the next day:

• Update your profile on LinkedIn so that your summary statement articulates your competitive advantages. You should be able to fill in this sentence: "Because of my [skill/experience/strength], I can do [type of professional work] better than [specific types of other professionals in my industry]."

• How would *other* professionals you work with fill in the above sentence (i.e., describe your competitive advantage)? If there's a gap, you either have a self-judgment problem, or a marketing problem.

In the next week:

• Identify three people who are striving toward aspirations similar to your own. Use them as benchmarks. What are *their* differentiators? How did they get to where they are? Bookmark their LinkedIn profiles, subscribe to their blogs and tweets. Track their professional evolution and take inspiration and insight from their journeys.

• Go on LinkedIn or Twitter, search for your employer and other companies you're interested in, and "follow" each of them. This will make it easier to track the emergence of new opportunities and risks.

• Write down some of your key assets in the context of a market reality. BAD: I excel at public speaking. GOOD: I excel at public speaking on engineering topics, relative to how good most engineers are at public speaking.

In the next month:

• Review your calendar, journals, and old emails and get a sense for how you spent your last six Saturdays. What do you do when you have nothing urgent to do? How you spend your free time may reveal your true interests and aspirations; compare them to what you *say* your aspirations are.

• Think about how you're currently adding value at work. If you stopped going to the office suddenly, what would not get done? What's a day in the life of your company with you not there? That may be where you're adding value. Think about the things people frequently compliment you on—those may be your strengths.

• Create a soft-asset investment plan that emphasizes learning about growth markets and growth opportunities. Maybe this means taking a trip to China, attending a conference on clean technology, or signing up for a software programming course. Email your plan to three trusted connections and ask them to hold you accountable. Budget money to pay for these things, if necessary.

Network Intelligence

Meet with three trusted connections and ask them what they see as your greatest strengths. If they had to come to you for help or advice on one topic, what would it be?

3

Plan to Adapt

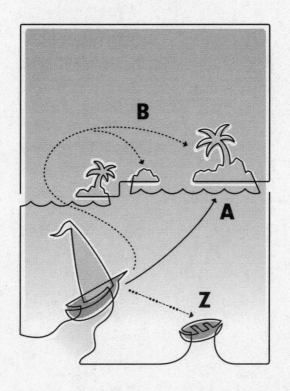

The bestselling career book of all time goes by the whimsical name *What Color Is Your Parachute?* But when it comes to charting a career plan, that's the wrong question. What you should be asking yourself is whether your parachute can keep you aloft in changing conditions. The unfortunate truth is that in today's career landscape, your parachute—no matter its color—may be shredded and tattered. And if it isn't that way already, it could get that way at any time.

In his first chapter, *Parachute* author Richard Bolles writes, "It is important, before you enter the job hunt, to decide exactly what you are looking for—whether you call it your passion, or your purpose in life, or your mission. . . . *Passion first, job-hunt later*."[1] After four decades in print, this is still the accepted wisdom today. You see similar advice all over. Habit number two of Stephen Covey's *Seven Habits of Highly Effective People* is, "Begin with the end in mind": you should produce a personal mission statement that puts your goals in focus. In *The Purpose-Driven Life*, Rick Warren advances the idea that each of us has a God-given purpose for being on this planet.

The primary message of these books (of which there are

more than 50 million copies in circulation) and countless others is to listen to your heart and follow your passion. Find your true north by filling out worksheets or engaging in deep, thoughtful introspection. Once you've got a mission in mind, these books urge, you're supposed to develop a long-term plan for fulfilling it. You're supposed to craft detailed, specific goals. You're urged to figure out who you are and where you want to be in ten years, and then work backward to develop a roadmap for getting there.

This philosophy has some serious strengths. It's important to have worthy aspirations. If you are passionate about something, you'll have fun, stay committed, and achieve more. It's also right to invest for the long term: to find out whether you're good at something and whether you like it, you need to stick with it for a meaningful amount of time.

But while these strengths may have made them the right philosophies in past decades, today there are some *huge* problems with this approach to career planning. First, it presumes a static world, and as we saw in Chapter 1, the career landscape isn't what it used to be. Deciding where you want to be in ten years and then formulating a plan for getting there might work if our environments were unchanging. It might work if getting from point A to point B in your career were like crossing a lake in a boat on a calm summer's day. But you're not in a calm lake. You're in a chaotic ocean. Conventional career planning can work under conditions of relative stability, but in times of uncertainty and rapid change, it is severely limiting, if not dangerous. You will change. The environment around you will change. Your allies and competitors will change.

Second, this philosophy presumes that fixed, accurate self-knowledge can be easily attained. In fact, lofty questions about identity and moral purpose, along with deceptively simple ones like "What am I passionate about?" take time to work out, and the answers frequently change. It's unwise, no matter your stage of life, to try to pinpoint a single dream around which your existence revolves.

Third, as we learned in the last chapter, just because your heart comes alive at a calling doesn't mean someone will pay you to do it. If you can't find someone who wants to employ you to pursue your dream job, or if you can't financially sustain yourself—that is, earn a salary that allows you to live the lifestyle you prefer—then trying to turn your passion into a career doesn't really get you very far.

So which is it? Should you follow a plan or stay flexible? Should you listen to your heart or listen to the market? The answer is *both*. They're false choices—the same false choices entrepreneurs are frequently dealt. Entrepreneurs are told they must be really persistent in fulfilling their vision, but also be ready to change their business based on market feedback. They are told to do a business they're passionate about, but also to adapt to customer needs.

The successful ones do both. They are flexibly persistent: they start companies that are true to their values and vision, yet they remain flexible enough to adapt. They are obsessed with customer feedback, yet they also know when not to listen to their customers. They draw up light plans with the intent of developing true competitive advantage in the marketplace, but they're also nimble enough to stray from those plans when appropriate. And they are always driving toward developing true competitive advantage in the marketplace.

To run a successful start-up of you in today's world, you can—and must—do the same in planning your career. This chapter will show you how.

ADAPTIVE START-UPS, ADAPTIVE CAREERS

Flickr is one of the most widely used photo hosting and sharing websites, with an estimated five billion–plus images on its servers. But the company wasn't started by photography pros. In fact, its founders, Caterina Fake and Stewart Butterfield (who teamed up with Jason Classon), didn't set out to start a photo-sharing service at all.

Their original product, rolled out in 2002, was a multiplayer online game called Game Neverending. Most gaming platforms at that time allowed one or at most a few people to play the same game together at the same time. But Caterina and Stewart wanted to create a game that hundreds of people could play at the same time. To this end, the plan was to build something they saw less as a game and more as a "social space designed to facilitate and enable play." To attract and retain players to this social space, they pumped out social features like groups and instant messaging, including one add-on to the instant messenger application that allowed players to share photographs with one another. As with most features of the game, the photo-sharing add-on was developed very quickly—it only took eight weeks from idea to implementation.

When photo sharing was first added to Game Neverending in 2004, it was no big deal—photographs were just another thing players could trade with one another, like the objects they would collect during the course of the game. However, it didn't take long for the photo-sharing capability to eclipse the game itself in popularity. As this became increasingly apparent to the leadership team, they were faced with a decision: Should they try to expand their new photo-sharing platform while sticking to their long-term plan and continuing to develop Game Neverending, or should they put the game (and its twenty thousand avid users) on hold to devote the majority of their precious resources to photo sharing? They decided to deviate from the original plan and focus exclusively on building the photo application and the photo-sharing community that went along with it. They called it Flickr. (I invested just as it became the photo service.)

Flickr soon became the photo-sharing service of choice for millions of Internet users. Its social features—tagging and sharing—grew naturally out of the social DNA that defined the original online game, even as they differentiated the service in response to market feedback. In 2005 Yahoo! acquired the company, making it a Web 2.0 poster child. But more than just a Silicon Valley success story, the evolution of Flickr is a case study in smart adapting: its founders were in constant motion early on, tried many things to see what would work, and nimbly shifted their plans based on what they learned.

These are the very same strategies that define some of the most inspiring careers. Take, for example, Sheryl Sandberg. Today, Sheryl is chief operating officer of Facebook, where she is in charge of the company's business operations. She serves on the boards of Disney and Starbucks. *Fortune* named her one of the most powerful women in business.

You might think someone so successful knew her goals and aspirations from day one, and followed a rigorous and ambitious career plan to achieve them. But you'd be wrong. Sheryl hasn't stuck to a conventional career plan. In fact, as an idealistic undergraduate majoring in economics she never imagined that she would one day be working in the private sector, much less as a top executive for one of the world's most valuable companies. Sheryl began her career in India, about as far as one could get from Silicon Valley. There she went to work on public health projects for the World Bank. It was a first job consistent with deeply embedded values: to give back to those less fortunate and to make a difference in the world. Sheryl had grown up in a home where political activism was as normal as eating or breathing. Her father was a doctor who regularly took his family on vacations to Third World destinations, where he would provide surgical services for free to the poor. Sheryl's mother was involved in a movement to support Soviet dissidents by helping them smuggle into the USSR contraband white chocolate disguised as soap—which could then be sold on the black market for much-needed cash. Sheryl knew that she was lucky to have been born in the United States, with its freedom and wealth of opportunities, and she was driven by an intense desire to give back in some way.

Yet after a couple of years with the World Bank, Sheryl shifted course and left the public sector to enroll at Harvard

Business School, where she earned an MBA. From academia, her next stop was the business world. But after a one-year stint at management consulting firm McKinsey, she realized the corporate career track wasn't for her; so she shifted yet again, this time to Washington, DC, where she served as then U.S. Secretary of Treasury Larry Summers's chief of staff from 1996 through 2001. It wasn't providing health care to the impoverished of India, but she was helping to shape policy in ways that would have a meaningful effect on the lives of many Americans. (It should be noted that working for Summers wasn't an accident: he had been her economics professor in college and had also hired her at the World Bank. As always, Sheryl was thoughtfully tapping her connections to find the next opportunity, something we talk more about later.)

After President Clinton left office, Sheryl asked then Google CEO Eric Schmidt, whom she had met at Treasury, for advice on her next career move. She recalls Schmidt's reaction as she made a detailed presentation of the pros and cons of her various options: "No, no! Get out of the weeds. Go where there's fast growth, because fast growth creates all opportunities,"[2] he told her. It was outstanding advice: Work in a market with natural momentum. Ride the big waves.

As it turned out, in 2002 Google was that place. Schmidt made Sheryl an offer. She accepted and became Google's vice president of global online sales and operations. She grew the company's online sales and operations group from four individuals in California to a global team of thousands of people and played crucial roles in developing and growing both of

Google's online advertising programs, AdWords and Ad-Sense, still the sources of the majority of Google's revenues.

Shifting from the public to the private sector, from the high-powered corridors of Washington, DC, to the organized chaos of Silicon Valley, might strike you as abrupt, or even random. But in fact, each move made sense given the interplay of her assets, aspirations, and the market realities. Her honed management skills would be useful for a fast-growing company; her economics background would help develop a sales model for a new type of online advertising; and Google's mission was rooted in making the world a better place. After six years at Google, Mark Zuckerberg hired Sheryl to be COO at Facebook, where she remains today.

What Flickr and Sheryl have in common is that they each challenge common assumptions about the path to success. Flickr contradicts the idea that winning start-ups come out of nowhere and ride the founders' brilliant idea to take over the world. In reality, most companies don't execute a single brilliant master plan. They go through stops and starts, a couple near-death experiences, and a great deal of adaptation. Pixar started as a company that sold a special computer for doing digital animation; it took a while till they got into the moviemaking business. Similarly, Starbucks originally sold only coffee beans and coffee equipment; they hadn't planned to sell coffee by the cup.

Sheryl's story contradicts the analogous assumption that massively successful people find their calling at an early age, devise a bulletproof life plan, and then follow it unwaveringly until attainment. Sheryl's career plan wasn't something she crafted once in her early twenties and then followed blindly. She didn't assemble a bunch of dominos, knock over the first piece, and then sit back and watch the rest fall into place over time. Instead of locking herself in to a single career path, she evaluated new opportunities as they presented themselves, taking into consideration her (ever-growing) set of intellectual and experiential assets. She pivoted to new professional tracks without ever losing sight of what really mattered to her. "The reason I don't have a plan is because if I have a plan I'm limited to today's options," she says.[3]

Among some of the most notable professionals, she is the rule, not the exception. Sure, Bill Clinton decided on politics at age sixteen, and set his sights on the presidency almost as young. But most of us zig and zag our way through life. Tony Blair spent a year trying to make a go of it as a rock music promoter before entering politics. Jerry Springer was mayor of Cincinnati before attaining daytime television fame. Andrea Bocelli practiced law before he became a world-famous singer. Winning careers, like winning start-ups, are in permanent beta: always a work in progress.

It's important to understand, though, that while entrepreneurial companies and people are always evolving, the choices they're making are disciplined, not random. There is real *planning* going on, even if there are no firm *plans*. We call this kind of disciplined, adaptive planning ABZ Planning, and it's what we'll cover in the balance of the chapter.

ABZ PLANNING

ABZ Planning is the antidote to the "what color is your parachute" approach to career planning. It is an adaptive approach to planning that promotes trial and error. It allows you to aggressively pursue upside and mitigate against possible downside risks. ABZ Planning isn't something you do once early in your career. It's a process as important for someone in their forties or fifties as for a newly minted college grad. There is no beginning, middle, or end to a career journey; no matter how old you are or at what stage, you will always be planning and adapting.

So what do *A*, *B*, and *Z* refer to exactly? Plan A is what you're doing right now. It's your current implementation of your competitive advantage. Within a Plan A you make minor adjustments as you learn; you *iterate* regularly. Plan B is what you *pivot* to when you need to change either your goal or the route for getting there. Plan B tends to be in the same general ballpark as Plan A. Sometimes you pivot because Plan A isn't working; sometimes you pivot because you've discovered a new opportunity that's just better than what you're doing now. In either case, don't write out an elaborate Plan B—things will change too much after the ink dries—but do give thought to your parameters of motion and alternatives. Once you pivot to a Plan B and stick with it, that becomes your new Plan A. Twenty years ago Sheryl Sandberg's Plan A was the World Bank. Today, her Plan A is Facebook, because it's where she is right now.

Plan Z is the fallback position: your lifeboat. In business and life, you always want to keep playing the game. If failure means you end up on the street, that's an unacceptable failure. So what's your certain, reliable, stable plan if all your career plans go to hell or if you want to do a major life change? That's Plan Z. The certainty of Plan Z is what allows you to take on uncertainty and risk in your Plans A and B.

Later in the chapter we'll go into more detail about each of these stages, but first we want to offer some general tips that apply at all stages of your career plan—whether it's A, B, or even Z.

Make Plans Based on Your Competitive Advantage

Career plans should leverage your assets, set you in the direction of your aspirations, and account for the market realities. The problem is, as we learned in the last chapter, these three puzzle pieces are always changing. The best you can do is articulate educated hypotheses about each. "I believe I am skilled at X, I believe I want to do Y, I believe the market needs Z." *All* plans contain these sorts of assumptions; good ones make them explicit so that you can track them over time. Essentially, you want to make explicit the things that need to be true for your plan to work. These hypotheses should lead you to specific actions. Companies often have broad missions like maximizing shareholder value, but as Jack Welch has said, maximizing shareholder value "is not a strategy that tells you what to do when you come to work every day."[4] Similarly, you may have broad aspirations, like "help interesting people do interesting things" or "design human ecosystems." But real planning means plotting the specific steps it will take to make those aspirations happen.

Prioritize Learning

Many people defer collecting full-time wages by spending twenty-three consecutive years in school. A high school drop-out can make more money in the short run than the guy stuck studying chemistry. But in the long run, the logic goes, a person with a foundation of knowledge and skills will make more money and most likely live a more meaningful life. It's true. And there's a similar belief in start-ups: technology companies focus on learning over profitability in the early years to maximize revenue in the later years.

Unfortunately, for far too many, focused learning ends at college graduation. They read about stocks and bonds instead of reading books that improve their mind. They compare their cash salary to their peers' instead of comparing lessons learned. They invest in the stock market and neglect investing in themselves. They focus, in short, on hard assets instead of soft assets. This is a mistake. We're not suggesting you be a starving, unshaven graduate student forever; you do need to earn money and build economic assets. But as much as you can, prioritize plans that offer the best chance at learning about yourself and the world. Not only will you make more money in the long run, but your career journey will be more fulfilling. Ask yourself, "Which plan will grow my soft assets the fastest?" Even simpler: "Which plan offers the most learning potential?"

Learn by Doing

Entrepreneurs penetrate the fog of the unknown by testing their hypotheses through trial and error. Any entrepreneur (and any expert on cognition/learning) will tell you that practical knowledge is best developed by doing, not just thinking or planning. At Flickr, there was an assumption that a multiplayer online game would have the most uptake. It was only by launching it, gauging user feedback, and building new side features like photo sharing every several weeks, that the team learned where the real opportunity lay. In the early days of LinkedIn, the plan was to have members invite their trusted connections by email—an invitation mechanism would fuel membership growth. But it turned out that the best way to enable viral spread was actually to enable members to upload their address books and see who else was on the service already.

For careers, too, you don't know what the best plan is until you try. It was only after I spent time in that graduate program that I learned academia wasn't the path for me. When I moved to the business world, I mistakenly thought my competitive advantage was being able to hold complexity in my head and master abstractions. But when I started *working*, I discovered my real advantage in the Internet industry was having the ability to think simultaneously about individual psychology and social dynamics on a massive scale.

Learn by doing. Not sure if you can break into the phar-
maceutical industry? Spend six months interning at Pfizer
making connections and see what happens. Curious whether
marketing or product development is a better fit than what you
currently do? If you work in a company where those functions
exist, offer to help out for free. Whatever the situation, *actions,*
not plans, generate lessons that help you test your hypotheses
against reality. Actions help you discover where you want to
go and how to get there.

Make Reversible, Small Bets

Occasional missteps are to be expected when you take this
experimental approach to career planning. It's the "error"
part of trial and error. But these errors needn't be permanent. Good Plan A's can be stopped or reversed or morphed
into a Plan B. A good Plan A minimizes the cost of failure.
Don't bet the farm. Iterate bit by bit, learn experience by experience. Start with a trial period. Keep your day job. ABZ
Planning embraces recoverable failure so long as it generates
real lessons.

Think Two Steps Ahead

Planning and adapting means thinking carefully about your
future. Lunging at the first well-paid and/or high-status job
you come upon may offer immediate gratification, but it won't
get you any closer to building a meaningful career. A goal
that can be achieved in a single step is probably not very

meaningful—or ambitious. The business professor Clayton Christensen once told graduating students at Harvard Business School, "If you study the root causes of business disasters, over and over you'll find [a] predisposition toward endeavors that offer immediate gratification." At the same time, though, don't do the opposite and think ahead too far in the future. Again, you will change, the world will change, the competition will change. It's why Plan C, Plan D, or Plan E are not part of this framework.

The best thing to do is to think and plan two steps ahead. If you'd like to be promoted from analyst to associate, it may mean a first step of building a relationship with a key partner, or taking a night course to pick up advanced financial management skills before taking that step of marching into the boss's office and asking for that promotion. Sometimes the first step toward a goal is rather simple. A question people sometimes ask us is, "What's the best way to get into Silicon Valley start-ups?" Well, there are various ways, but the first step is this: move here!

If you're unsure what your first, or even your second, step should be, pick a first step with high option value, meaning that it could lead to a broad range of options. Management consulting is a classic example of a career move that maximizes "optionality" because the skills and experiences of consulting can be helpful in and applied toward many other next steps, even if you're not sure what those steps are yet. A good Plan A is one that offers flexibility to pivot to a range of possible Plan B's; similarly, a good first step generates a large number of possible follow-on second steps.

Maintain an Identity Separate from Specific Employers

There was a great article in the *Onion* in November 2008 about how medical personnel had to be dispatched to help Obama campaign workers found lying on park benches and wandering city streets aimlessly, their lives devoid of meaning after election victory. It was a joke, of course, but it actually highlights a serious point: Throwing your heart into something is great, but when any one thing becomes all that you stand for, you're vulnerable to an identity crisis when you pivot to a Plan B. Establish an identity independent of your employer, city, and industry. For example, make the headline of your LinkedIn profile not a specific job title (e.g., "VP of Marketing at Company X") but personal-brand or asset-focused (e.g., "Entrepreneur. Product Strategist. Investor."). Start a personal blog and begin developing a public reputation and public portfolio of work that's not tied to your employer. This way, you'll have a professional identity that you can carry with you as you shift jobs. You own yourself. It's the start-up of *you*.

Now let's look at how you can apply all these strategies at different points along the A–B–Z timeline.

PLAN A: ALMOST READY, AIM, FIRE, AIM, FIRE, AIM, FIRE . . .

PayPal is the leading online-payments company, processing more than 20 percent of all e-commerce transactions in the

United States. People around the world have sent hundreds of billions of dollars to one another over the Web—instantly and safely—thanks to PayPal's innovative technology. When PayPal went public in 2002 (one of only two companies to do so that year), it gave hope to a technology industry in recession. When eBay acquired the company for $1.5 billion, PayPal staked its claim as a great Silicon Valley success story. Yet the PayPal Plan A did not look anything like the company looks today.

In 1998 programmer Max Levchin teamed with derivatives trader Peter Thiel to create a "digital wallet"—an encryption platform that allowed you to store cash and information securely on your mobile phone. That soon evolved to software that allowed you to send and receive digital cash wirelessly and securely via a Palm Pilot (the first of several iterations) so that two friends could split a dinner tab using their PDAs. It was a neat idea that leveraged Max's and Peter's technology and finance backgrounds, respectively (complementary assets that gave them a competitive edge as founders). Max and Peter named the company Confinity— a mix of *confidence* and *infinity*. But the Palm Pilot wasn't catching on.

So Max and Peter iterated again. They developed an online payment transfer service that didn't require a Palm or any other mobile phone application. It let you send money securely over the Web to anyone with an email address. Recipients could in turn transfer the money wirelessly to their checking accounts. To make the service, which they dubbed PayPal, even more useful to businesses, they added credit card processing. No merchant accounts needed to process a credit card payment: just a simple, universal online interface.

Confinity signed up early adopters for peer-to-peer money transfers on both the Palm Pilot application and the PayPal online payment transfer service, although not as quickly as expected for the Palm Pilot. The company struggled to find and articulate a mass-market use case; the general public was not accustomed to electronically and wirelessly sending cash to one another.

In short, PayPal's Plan A had played out. There were no more iterations to make, no more small bets to take. Many lessons had been learned. But the game wasn't over yet, thanks to an auction site called eBay that kept growing and growing. But more on that in a minute.

Somewhat earlier, I was at a similar crossroads in my career. My Plan A (after leaving academia) had been to go into the computer industry, but I had one big concern. I was unsure I had the technical skills to compete in a place like Silicon Valley. Creating technology that millions of people would use was an aspiration. There was clearly growing market demand for folks who had experience with the Internet. But did I have the skills, and could I make enough connections in the tech industry, to become a hitter? To find out, I *tried*. I got a job (via a friend of a friend) at Apple Computer in Cupertino.

Apple hired me into their user experience group, but shortly after starting on the job I learned that product/market fit—the focus of product management—mattered more than user experience or design. You can develop great and important user interfaces, and Apple certainly did, but if customers don't need or want the product, they won't buy. At Apple, and in most companies, the product/market fit questions fall under the purview of the product management group, not user experience. And because product management is vital in any product organization, work experience in the area tends to lead to more diverse career opportunities.

So, much in the way that the earliest version of PayPal iterated from a digital wallet to an online payment transfer service, I attempted to iterate into a product management role within Apple (Plan "A1"). But the product management jobs required product management experience. It's a common catch-22: for jobs that require prior experience, how do you get the experience the first time? My solution: do the job for free on the side. I sought out the head of product management within the eWorld group at Apple, James Isaacs, and told him I had a few product ideas. I offered to write them up in addition to everything else I was doing, and I did. Product managers reviewed my ideas and gave me feedback and encouragement. It was a small, reversible bet, an experiment within my job, and it worked well.

The experience taught me that I did indeed have the skills and intuitions to make a go of it in the tech industry (assets). I learned that product management was closer to the heart of technology companies than the job I was initially hired for (a market reality). And I learned that product strategy was a path that could propel me to the highest levels of seniority in the business world—which in turn would help me realize my vision of making a huge impact (aspirations). All important lessons I wouldn't have gained any way other than by setting foot in the industry.

After almost two years at Apple I left to go to Fujitsu in Silicon Valley to work as a full-time product manager (Plan A2). I was still on Plan A: I was still experimenting within the tech industry. But all the while I was honing my assets and aspirations for what I might like to do next: my Plan B.

PLAN B: PIVOT AS YOU LEARN

While you'll always be tinkering and adjusting your Plan A, should you decide you need to make a bigger change, that's when you pivot to Plan B. Pivoting isn't throwing a dart on the map and then going there. It's changing direction or changing your path to get somewhere *based on what you've learned along the way*.[5] Once you've pivoted and are on a new track, that becomes your new Plan A.

PayPal's pivot to Plan B happened because of eBay. At the time, eBay was the busiest person-to-person marketplace on the Web. Yet auctions demanded a person-to-person financial transaction. This meant that a buyer in one city usually mailed a check or money order to a seller in another city. This process was inconvenient, time-intensive, and unreliable. As eBay grew in size, sellers became increasingly frustrated with money-collection options. They wanted a more efficient way to accept payments.

When the PayPal team saw that growing numbers of eBay

users were trying to use PayPal to handle payments, the first reaction was "Why the heck are they using our product?!" (Remember, PayPal's first focus was on mobile payments.) That quickly turned into "Ooh—maybe those people are our customers!" Which in turn led to a realization that the company should pivot to Plan B: offer the eBay community an easy way to pay for the items they bought in online auctions. In 1999 PayPal ditched the Palm Pilot app (the original Plan A) and focused on eBay. Plan B wasn't something random, like an online chat application. It stayed true to PayPal's initial encryption roots while shifting to capitalize on what appeared to be the real market need.

As it happened, my career Plan B intersected with PayPal's Plan B. A few years before PayPal took off, after stints at Apple and Fujitsu, I had decided to pivot into the adjacent world of entrepreneurship and start a company of my own. In 1997 I cofounded Socialnet.com, an online dating site. At the time, my Plan A was Socialnet. On the side, I was helping Peter and Max get PayPal off the ground, promising to return their calls by midnight the same day and serving on their founding board of directors. In my mind, I had two possible Plan B's. One would be to deepen my relationship with PayPal—i.e., join full-time. Another would be to get a general job in the tech industry. My experiences cofounding Socialnet would make either career move a natural pivot. About a year before Socialnet closed down (an experience that taught me a tremendous amount), in January 2000, I decided to join Max and Peter full-time at PayPal and became executive vice president.

Both PayPal's Plan B and my own career Plan B worked out well. At PayPal, online payment processing for eBay users (and beyond!) was a big winner. This isn't to say it was smooth sailing the rest of the way; quite the opposite. PayPal changed its business model, brought on new executives, merged with another company, and endured millions of dollars of losses due to fraud. Probably the lowest point was when the company spent $12 million in cash in one month without a dime of revenue. (The situation was so dire that I pointed out to Peter at the time that we could spend a day throwing fistfuls of cash off the roof of a building and not come close to matching the company's burn rate.) The team flexibly dealt with—and learned from—these challenges while persistently pursuing the vision of delivering online payment transfer in multiple currencies.

From a career standpoint, I hit similar bumps in the road, but they were all instructive. I learned to adapt to the speed of the start-up world. I learned about how to attract and hire the right talent. I learned about the right and wrong kinds of impatience. And much more. What I learned from the PayPal experience equipped me for my next pivot: trying again to start my own company. That company was LinkedIn.

When to Pivot: To Pursue Upside or Avoid Downside

How do you know when to pivot from Plan A (what you're doing now) to a Plan B? When is it time to change divisions, change jobs, or even change the industry you work in? You'll rarely know for sure when to pivot or when to persist in what you're doing. In general, a lesson from the technology industry is that it's better to be in front of a big change than to be behind it. But the question of when to shift exactly is a question of both art and science, intuitive judgment combined with the best feedback or data you can collect—something we'll discuss in the network intelligence chapter. And of course expect both good luck and bad luck along the way that will open and close unexpected windows of opportunity.

The common presumption is that you shift to Plan B when something isn't working. That's frequently the case but not always. What you're doing now doesn't have to be failing for it to make sense to shift. Sheryl was hardly failing when she pivoted to the Google opportunity. If you find that the grass really is greener somewhere else, go there!

•   •   •

Of course, given the volatility of today's career landscape, the decision to pivot often isn't voluntary. Sometimes we're forced to go to Plan B. We could be fired, new technology could automate or offshore our routinized job, or the entire industry we work in could be disrupted. Or we might undergo a major life change, like having children, that reorders life priorities and necessitates a pivot into a situation that offers more work/life balance.

Andy Grove, the Intel cofounder, refers to these kinds of events as *inflection points*. In a business context, Grove says a strategic inflection point is what happens when a "10×" force (ten times bigger) disrupts a business. For example, for a small-town general store, a Walmart setting up shop nearby is a 10× force on the general store. For a midsize financial firm, a huge corporate takeover is a 10× force. Countless once-giants like Blockbuster, Kodak, and the *New York Times* are all in the midst of environmental inflection points brought about by the 10× force of the digital revolution.

In the same way that external forces threaten companies, so too can they have profound effects on your career. For an autoworker in Detroit, the closing of a major plant is a 10× force. For a public school teacher, the slashing of school budgets is a 10× force. As Grove says, "[A] career inflection point results from a subtle but profound shift in the operating environment, where the future of your career will be determined by the actions you take in response."[6] An inflection point at your company or industry usually will require you to either change your skills or change your environment. In other words, it will often require you to pivot.

It's impossible to know exactly when an inflection point will disrupt your career. The only thing you can safely know about the future is that it will be sooner and stranger than you think. So instead of trying to do the impossible and *predict* when an inflection point will threaten, *prepare* for the unknown. Build up your soft assets and proactively embrace new technology so that if and when the inflection point does come, you are ready to swiftly parlay skills into a Plan B.

James Gaines is a model example of someone who has adapted his plans in anticipation of disruptive forces. During the reign of print magazines, Gaines was king. He was managing editor of *People* magazine, then *Life* magazine, and finally

Time magazine—at the time, one of the most influential print publications in the world. There, he interviewed heads of state and directed an editorial staff of more than six hundred journalists. He left the magazine in 1996 to run the corporate editorial side of the Time Inc. empire, sharing oversight of the company's twenty-six magazine operations. A year of that reminded him that writing—not management—was his passion. So he went independent and began writing books. Since he could write from anywhere, he moved his family to Paris to provide a more colorful upbringing for his children and a more inspiring backdrop for his writing.

While living in Paris in 2002, Gaines and his son went to see the first Harry Potter film. That night turned out to be a pivotal career experience for Gaines. In one scene, Harry opens a book and a three-dimensional human face leaps out of the page and wiggles its face. Gaines recalls the scene triggering an epiphany: an interactive book! At the time, he was writing a book about Johann Sebastian Bach and he found it frustrating that the reader couldn't hear the music described in the text. Perhaps technology could transform books for the better; perhaps it could add a touch of Potter magic to the reader experience.

By the summer of 2008, just shy of his sixty-first birthday, Gaines moved back to the United States with two published books to his name. With a lifetime of print journalism and publishing experience, he could have held any number of senior posts in the trade. But he saw that the future had arrived and that old media may not have a place in it. So he pivoted to Plan B. He was excited, not panicked. Rather than mourn the past, he embraced the unique storytelling possibilities of a digital canvas. This positive mind-set sustained him during his learning curve.

He went on to become editor in chief of *Flyp*, a start-up online magazine that produced video and audio narratives on politics, finance, and social issues. At an online, multimedia magazine, Gaines had a lot to learn. And there was no formal training or classes. His youthful *subordinates* were his on-the-job *teachers*, instructing him on how to do video editing, audio editing, understand MySQL databases, and learn the pros and cons of other Internet protocols. To hear Gaines tell it, you'd think picking up these new skills was a piece of cake. But think about his ego. He had decades of experience. A long list of accomplishments. Yet he found himself, in a sense, powerless and young again. It was Day 1 for Gaines. He was in permanent beta.

Instead of waiting for an inflection point to disrupt his career, Gaines adapted. Rather than try to preserve what has always been, Gaines parlayed his skills into new media. Throughout, he never lost sight of his competitive advantage in the career marketplace: his ability to tell stories that move people, regardless of the medium.

Where to Pivot: To an Adjacent Niche, Something Different but Related

Flickr's Plan A was an online multiplayer game. My original career Plan A was to be an academic. Sheryl's was to help the underprivileged, starting in India. James Gaines's was to be a magazine editor. None is on the original plan now, and at first glance the current plans seem unrelated; but if you look closely you'll see a logical evolution through the various pivots. I am still spreading knowledge and ideas about social life through LinkedIn, through the companies I choose to fund, and now through this book with Ben. Sheryl is still helping the underprivileged in places like Syria and Egypt who are using Facebook to organize and rally against oppressive governments. *The best Plan B is different but very much related to what you're already doing.* As you think about your own Plan B alternatives, favor options that let you keep one foot planted while the other one swings to the new territory. Pivot into an adjacent niche.

How to Pivot: Start It on the Side

Unless you need to take immediate action, one way to begin the process of pivoting is to start your potential Plan B on the side. Start learning a skill during the evenings and weekends. Start building relationships with people who work in an adjacent industry. Apply for a part-time internship. Start a side consulting practice. This is what I did when I began advising PayPal while still working at Socialnet: it was a side project that had the potential to become a full-blown Plan B later on (which it ultimately did).

Companies ranging from 3M to Gore-Tex, Google to LinkedIn, pay employees to spend a portion of their time experimenting on side projects. Why not make this a personal career policy? Set aside one day a week or month or even every few months to work on something that could be part of your Plan B. If you have a business idea you want to pursue, a skill you want to learn, a relationship you want to form, or some other curiosity or aspiration, start on it as a side project and see where it goes. At a minimum, just start talking to people. Take a day and arrange five coffee meetings with people who work in an adjacent industry.

If you want an even smaller baby step, take a "vocation vacation." A company by the same name lets you test-drive dream jobs—whether it's being a symphony composer or a real estate broker or a travel writer. If you think you might like to open your own spa business, for example, they'll connect you with a spa owner in Texas and fly you out to spend two days with her, observing the ins and outs of the business and discussing in depth what it takes to succeed in the industry. It's a great way to explore potential Plan B's without making a big or irreversible commitment.

PLAN Z: JUMP ON YOUR LIFEBOAT AND REGROUP

The reason many people do not embrace trial and error, learning by doing, adaptation, and the other themes of this chapter is because these strategies introduce real uncertainty. It's easy to say "learn by doing"—but what if you're not sure *what* you'll learn or *what* you should do? As we'll talk about in the risk chapter, uncertainty never goes away. Fear of failure never goes away. The way to feel comfortable with these entrepreneurial strategies is to have one plan in your life that's highly certain. That's Plan Z: a reliable plan you shift to when you no longer have confidence in Plan A and B, or when your plans get severely disrupted. The certainty of the Plan Z backstop is what enables you to be aggressive—not tentative—about Plans A and B. With a Plan Z, you'll at least know you can *tolerate* failure. Without it, you could be frozen in fear contemplating the worst-case scenarios.

When I started my first company, my father offered up an extra room in his house in the event it didn't work out—living there and finding a job somewhere else to earn money was my Plan Z. This allowed me to be aggressive in my entrepreneurial pursuits, as I knew I could draw my assets down to zero if necessary and still have a roof over my head. Becoming homeless or bankrupt or permanently unemployable is an unacceptable outcome when one of your career plans fails. Your Plan Z is there to prevent these unacceptable outcomes from becoming realities.

If you're in your twenties and single, getting a job at Starbucks and moving back in with your parents might be a viable Plan Z. If you're in your thirties or forties with children, on the other hand, it might mean cashing in your 401(k). Whatever it is for you, think of it as a lifeboat, not a long-term plan. Invoking Plan Z should allow you to retreat, regroup, and develop an entirely new Plan A. It's not an endpoint—it's what will keep you afloat while you reload and then relaunch yourself on a brand-new voyage, a brand-new Plan A.

INVEST IN YOURSELF

In the next day:

• Make a list of your key uncertainties, doubts, and questions you have about your career at the present moment. Make a list of the hypotheses you're developing around these uncertainties—what are the things you're looking for to figure out whether you should stick with your Plan A, or pivot to Plan B?

• Write out your current Plan A and Plan Z, and jot some notes about what possible Plan B moves might be in your current situation.

In the next week:

• Schedule a coffee meeting with someone who used to work in your professional niche who pivoted to a new career plan. How did he or she make the shift? Why? Was it a good move? What were the signs that the time was right?

• Make a plan to develop more transferable skills, those skills and experiences that are broadly useful to potential other jobs. Writing skills, general management experience, technical and computer skills, people smarts, and international experience or language skills are examples of skills with high option value—that is, they are transferable to a wide range of possible Plan B's. Once you've figured out which transferable skills to invest in, make a concrete action plan you can stick to, whether by signing up for a course or conference, or simply by pledging to spend one hour each week self-learning.

In the next month:

- Begin on an experimental side project that you work on during some nights and weekends. Orient it around a skill or experience that is different but related—something that either enhances what you do now or can serve as a possible Plan B if your Plan A doesn't work out. Ideally, collaborate on this project with someone else in your network.

- Establish an identity independent of your employer, city, industry. Reserve a personal domain name (yourname.com). Print up a second set of business cards with just your name on it and a personal email address.

Network Intelligence

Reach out to five people who work in adjacent niches and ask them to coffee. Compare your plans with theirs. Keep up these relationships over time so you can access diverse information and so you're in a better position to potentially pivot to those niches when necessary.

4

It Takes a Network

ven if you realize the fact that you are in permanent beta, even if you develop a competitive advantage, even if you adapt your career plans to changing conditions—even if you do these things but do so *alone*—you'll fall short. World-class professionals build networks to help them navigate the world. No matter how brilliant your mind or strategy, if you're playing a solo game, you'll always lose out to a team. Athletes need coaches and trainers, child prodigies need parents and teachers, directors need producers and actors, politicians need donors and strategists, scientists need lab partners and mentors. Penn needed Teller. Ben needed Jerry. Steve Jobs needed Steve Wozniak. Indeed, teamwork is eminently on display in the start-up world. Very few start-ups are started by only one person. Everyone in the entrepreneurial community agrees that assembling a talented team is as important as it gets.

Venture capitalists invest in people as much as in ideas. VCs will frequently back stellar founders with a so-so idea over mediocre founders with a good idea, on the belief that smart and adaptable people will maneuver their way to something that works. (We described this with PayPal and Flickr earlier in the book.) Not only should the founders be talented, they should be committed to getting other talented people on board. The strength of the cofounders and early employees reflects the individual strength of the CEO; that's why investors don't evaluate the CEO in isolation from his or her team. Vinod Khosla, cofounder of Sun Microsystems and a Silicon Valley investor, says, "The team you build is the company you build." Mark Zuckerberg says he spends half his time recruiting.

Just as entrepreneurs are always recruiting and building a team of stunning people, you want to always be investing in your professional network to grow the start-up that is your career. Quite simply, if you want to accelerate your career, you need the help and support of others. Of course, unlike company founders, you aren't hiring a fleet of employees who report to you, nor do you report to a board of directors. What you are doing—what you should be doing—is establishing a diverse team of allies and advisors with whom you grow over time.

Relationships matter to your career no matter the organization or level of seniority because every job boils down to interacting with people. In fact, the word *company* is derived from the Latin *cum* and *pane,* which means "breaking bread together."[1] Yes, even if you're a solo software coder, you'll still have to work with other people at some point, if you want to create a product people will actually use. Amazon, Boeing, UNICEF, and Whole Foods—to pick a handful of companies—are very different organizations, but they are all, ultimately, people organizations. *People* develop the technologies, write the mission statements, and stand behind the corporate logos and abstractions.

People are the source of key resources, opportunities, information, and the like. For example, my long-term friendship with Peter Thiel, which started in college, is what connected me to PayPal. Without the relationship, Peter never would have called me with the life-changing opportunity. Likewise, without the alliance, I wouldn't have referred Sean Parker and Mark Zuckerberg to Peter during Facebook's initial financing. In alliances, resources and assistance flow both ways.

People also act as gatekeepers. Jeffrey Pfeffer, professor of organizational behavior at Stanford, has marshaled evidence that shows that when it comes to getting promoted in your job, strong relationships and being on good terms with your boss can matter more than competence. This is not nefarious nepotism or politics (though unfortunately sometimes it's that). There's a good reason: a slightly less-competent person who gets along with others and contributes on a team can be better for the company than somebody who's 100 percent competent but isn't a team player.

Finally, relationships matter because the people you spend time with shape who you are and who you become. Behavior and beliefs are contagious: you easily "catch" the emotional state of your friends, imitate their actions, and absorb their values as your own.[2] If your friends are the types of people who get stuff done, chances are you'll be that way, too. *The fastest way to change yourself is to hang out with people who are already the way you want to be.*

I^{We} (I to the We): You and Your Team

Despite the fact that nothing important in life is done alone, we live in a hero-obsessed culture. If you survey the population on how a company of note like General Electric achieved its behemoth status, you'll probably hear about Jack Welch, but not a peep about the team he built around him. And if you ask about the career of a person like Jack Welch, you'll hear he got to the top of the totem pole because of things like hard work, intelligence, and creativity.

Typically, all kinds of *individual* attributes pepper explanations of a person's success. Books that promise to improve your life are shelved under "*self*-help." Seminars that promise to teach you how to be successful are considered *personal* development. Business schools rarely teach relationship-building skills. It's all about me, me, me, me. Why do we rarely talk about the friends, allies, and colleagues who make us who we are?

In part it's because the idea of a self-made man makes for a good story, and stories are how we process a messy, complex world. Good stories have a beginning, middle, and end; drama; clear causation; a hero and a villain. It's easier to tell stories that neglect the surrounding cast. *Superman and His Ten Allies* doesn't quite roll off the tongue as easily as *Superman*. We've been telling and retelling stories like these for centuries. Benjamin Franklin himself "artfully constructed his *Autobiography* as dazzling lessons in self-making."[3] Americans are particularly eager to embrace the self-made-man story because we are a country that has long celebrated the ideal of a guns-blazing John Wayne and the rugged individualism he stood for.

But tidy narratives tend to be misleading. In actuality, Franklin's networks and relationships were a huge part of his life, and played a huge part in his success. Indeed, if you study the life of any notable person, you'll find that the main character operates within a web of support. As tempting as it is to believe that we are the sole heroes of our own stories, we are enmeshed in cities, companies, fraternities, families, society at large—collections of people who shape us, help us, and yes, sometimes even hurt us. It is impossible to dissociate an individual from the environment of which he is a part. No story of achievement should ever be removed from its broader social context.

The self-made man may be a myth, but the old saw "There is no *I* in *team*" is wrong, too. There *is* an *I* in *team*. A team is made up of individuals with different strengths and abilities. Michael Jordan needed his team, but no one would dispute that he was more crucial to the success of the Chicago Bulls than his teammates. And one bad apple on an otherwise top-notch team can spoil the whole bunch. Research shows that a team in the business world will tend to perform at the level of the worst individual team member.[4] Your individual talent and hard work may not be sufficient for success, but it's absolutely necessary.

The nuanced version of the story of success is that both the individual and team matter. "I" vs. "We" is a false choice. It's both. Your career success depends on both your individual capabilities and your network's ability to magnify them. Think of it as I^{We}. An individual's power is raised exponentially with the help of a team (a network). But just as zero to the one hundredth power is still zero, there's no team without the individual.

This book is titled *The Start-up of You*. Really, the "you" is at once singular and plural.

Context Matters: Relationship Building in Professional Life

"Relationship" can mean many things. It can be long distance or proximate, project only or long term, emotionally close or purely professional. There are bosses, coworkers, colleagues, and subordinates. There are friends, neighbors, family members, and long-lost acquaintances. There are people you relate to out of love, out of friendship, out of respect, and out of necessity. There are people you work with based on a detailed contract that legally specifies roles and responsibilities; there are people you work with where nothing is written down. The universality of the word *relationship* makes sense: the essence of how human beings relate to one another transcends situational differences.

That said, there *are* key differences in how relationships function based on the context. There are people you know solely in a *personal* context. These include close personal friends and family. These are the people you call on a Saturday night, but not on a busy Monday morning at work. These are your childhood, high school, or college friends who may be dear to you but are not necessarily on an even remotely similar career trajectory. These are the people with whom a shared spirituality and alignment of core values may matter. Online, you connect with these friends and family on Facebook. You share photos of last night's party and play CityVille or Texas Hold'Em. Your Facebook profile picture might be kooky, and whether you are single or in a relationship is a point of interest for all.

Then there are those you know solely in a *professional* context. These include colleagues, industry acquaintances, customers, allies, business advisors, and service providers like your accountant or lawyer. You email these folks from your work address, and maybe not your personal Yahoo or Gmail account. Shared business goals and professional interests bring you together. Online, LinkedIn is where you connect with these trusted colleagues and valued acquaintances whom you recommend for jobs, collaborate with on professional projects, and tap for industry advice. It's where you share detailed information about your skill sets and work experience. Your head shot is professional. No one cares who you are or are not dating on LinkedIn. While most people have a small circle of close friends, they maintain a large circle of these valued acquaintances and colleagues.

Generally, you know people primarily in a personal *or* a professional context. The simple reason is etiquette and expectations. It's awkward if a coworker confesses marital infidelity while standing around the proverbial water cooler. (Cue a scene from the TV show *The Office* . . .) And your idea of a fun weekend might not involve playing in a sandbox with your coworker's kids. The more important reason why personal and professional are separate relates to conflict of loyalties. For example, suppose a coworker you consider a personal friend is screwing up on a big work project. If you don't speak up, you will be letting down other team members and your company as a whole, therefore hurting the project and your professional reputation at the same time. If you do speak up, your friend may resent you. Or suppose a personal friend asks you to be a reference on a prestigious job application, but you don't think he's truly qualified. It can strain the friendship. For these reasons, it can be tricky to ask close personal friends for career help because you're asking them to negotiate dueling loyalties: their duties as a professional and their duties as a friend.

Now, it's good to be friends with someone you work with. It's more fun. You may invite your coworker to your wedding. You may go winetasting with your boss and direct report over the weekend. You may link with some people on both Facebook *and* LinkedIn. But even in these cases, the vast majority of the time there will be limits to how much the friendship can flourish. And context will continue to govern etiquette and expectations. You say and do different things when at a bar on a Saturday night than when in the office on a Wednesday afternoon, even if you're with the exact same friends.

This chapter focuses on relationships that make you a more competitive business-of-one in a *professional context*. In other words, this is about professional relationships, and those personal friendships that also function in a professional context.

BUILD GENUINE RELATIONSHIPS

Many people are turned off by the topic of networking. They think it feels slimy, inauthentic. Go figure. Picture the consummate networker: the high-energy fast talker who collects as many business cards as he can, attends networking mixers in the evenings, sports slicked-back hair. Or the overambitious kid in your graduating class from college who frantically emails alumni, goes to cocktail parties with the board of trustees to schmooze, and adds anyone he's ever met as a friend on online social networks. These people are drunk on networking Kool-Aid and await a potential nasty social and professional hangover. Luckily, building and strengthening your network doesn't have to be like this.

Old-school "networkers" are transactional. They pursue relationships thinking only about what other people can do for them. And they'll only network with people when they need something, like a job or new clients. Relationship builders, on the other hand, try to help other people first. They don't keep score. They're aware that many good deeds get reciprocated, but they're not calculated about it. And they think about their relationships all the time, not just when they need something.

Networkers think it's important to have a really big address book. This emphasis on quantity means they perhaps unknowingly form mostly weak relationships. Relationship builders prioritize high-quality relationships over a large number of connections.

Networkers focus on tactical ways to meet new people. They think about how to dominate a cocktail party or how to cold-call an important person in their field. Relationship builders start by understanding how their existing relationships constitute a social network, and they meet new people through people they already know.

True relationship building in the professional world is like dating. When you're deciding whether or not to build a professional relationship with someone, there are many considerations: whether you like him or her; the capacity for the person to help you build your assets, reach your aspirations, and position you well competitively, and for you to help back in all the same ways; whether the person is adaptable and could help you adapt your career plan as necessary. And, like with dating, you should always have a long-term perspective.

Empathize and Help First

Building a genuine relationship with another person depends on (at least) two things. The first is seeing the world from the other person's perspective. No one knows this better than the skilled entrepreneur. Entrepreneurs succeed when they make stuff people will pay money for, which means understanding what's going on in the heads of customers. Discovering what people want, in the words of start-up investor Paul Graham, "deals with the most difficult problem in human experience: how to see things from other people's point of view, instead of thinking only of yourself."[5] Likewise, in relationships, it's only when you truly put yourself in the other person's shoes that you begin to develop an honest connection. This is tough. Whereas entrepreneurs have some ways of measuring how well they understand their customers by ultimately watching sales rise and fall, in day-to-day social life there's no such immediate feedback. Compounding that challenge is the fact that the basic way we perceive and process the external world makes us feel like everything revolves around us. The late writer David Foster Wallace once noted this literal truth: "There is no experience you have had that you are not the absolute center of. The world as you experience it is there in front of *you* or behind *you*, to the left or right of *you*, on *your* TV or *your* monitor."[6]

The second requirement is thinking about how you can help and collaborate with the other person rather than thinking about what *you* can *get* from him or her. When you come into contact with a successful person it's natural to immediately think, "What can this person do for me?" If you were to have a chance meeting with Tony Blair, we can't blame you for thinking about how you could get your photo taken with him. If you were to share a cab ride with a person of unusual wealth, it's natural to think about trying to convince her to donate or invest in one of your causes. We're not suggesting you be so saintly that a self-interested thought never crosses your mind. What we're saying is you should let go of those easy thoughts and think about how *you* can help *first*. (And only later think about what help you can ask for in return.) A study on negotiation found that a key difference between skilled negotiators and average negotiators was the time spent searching for shared interests, asking questions of the other person, and forging common ground. The effective negotiators spent more time doing these things—thinking about ways the other person would truly benefit as opposed to just trying to drive a hard bargain out of pure self-interest.[7] Do the same. Start with a friendly gesture toward the other person and genuinely mean it. (Later in the chapter we'll show exactly how to help.)

Dale Carnegie's classic book on relationships, despite all its wisdom, is unfortunately titled *How to Win Friends and Influence People*. This makes Carnegie widely misunderstood. You don't "win" a friend. A friend is not an asset you own; it's a shared relationship. A friend is an ally, a collaborator. Think of it like ballroom dancing. You don't control the other person's feet. Your task is to move in unison, perhaps gently guiding or following. There's a deep sense of mutuality. Trying to win/acquire friends as if they were objects undermines the endeavor altogether.

Now, few would cop to charges that they are trying to "acquire" relationships in this manner. Yet, their actions and behaviors indicate otherwise, and their relationships suffer as a result. Sometimes they are giving off a bad impression by trying too hard to *seem* genuine and caring. When you can tell someone is *attempting* sincerity it leaves you cold. It is like the feeling you have when someone says your first name all the time in conversation and you know he's been reading Carnegie. Or the feeling you get after reading networking books that stress being "authentic" but in the process make networking seem like a game that serves one's crass individual ambition. Novelist Jonathan Franzen gets it right when he says inauthentic people are obsessed with authenticity. Unless the process of bonding and allying with others comes off as effortlessly as tying your shoes, which is to say, unless allying and helping really *is* what you want to be doing, the collaborative mind-set will fail, and so, ultimately, will the relationship.

In a sentence, as you meet your friends and new people, shift from asking yourself the very natural question of "What's in it for me?" and ask instead, "What's in it for *us*?" All follows from that.

The Fun Factor

If it's not the sliminess of networking that turns some people away from the topic, it's the presumption that building relationships in a professional context is like flossing: you're told it is important, but it's no fun. When you see relationship building as a chore, you're more likely to go through the motions, be transactional (check the box on your to-do list), and acquire phony relationships as a result. This will make you ever more cynical, which results in even more phoniness. A vicious loop. It doesn't have to be this way.

Think about some of your happiest memories. Were you alone? Or were you surrounded by friends or family? Think about some of your most adventurous, stimulating experiences. Were you alone, or with others? Building relationships should be *fun*. That's how we think about it. Ben and I love the complexity of human interactions. We get excited at the prospect of working with others—it enlarges the sense of what's possible and expands the box in which we think.

(In fact, that's why this book is the result of a collaboration.) We're not suggesting you have to be an extrovert or life of the party. We just think it's possible to appreciate the mystery of another person's life experience. Building relationships is the thrilling if delicate quest to at once understand another person and allow that person to understand you.

THE STRUCTURE AND STRENGTH OF YOUR EXISTING NETWORK

This chapter is not about how to work a room or how to follow up after getting someone's business card. We're not going to tell you how to cold-call. That's because the best way to engage new people is via *the people you already know*. According to the National Health and Social Life Survey, 70 percent of Americans meet their spouse through someone they know, while only 30 percent meet after a self-introduction.[8] In a professional context, we would guess the numbers are even stronger in favor of introductions from existing connections.

So if you want to build a strong network that will help you move ahead in your career, it's vital to first take stock of the connections you already have. And not just because your existing connections will introduce you to new ones. Your network is influencing you as we speak, changing how you think and act, and opening and closing certain career doors—sometimes without your even knowing it.

There are various types of relationships in personal and professional contexts, from intimate friends and family to polite coworker contacts to medium-strength trust connections. Each type of relationship is different. We're going to focus on two types of relationships that matter in a professional context.

The first is professional allies. Who would be in your corner in a conflict or when you come under stress? Whom do you invite to dinner to brainstorm career options? Whom do you trust and proactively try to work with if you can? From whom do you solicit feedback on key projects? Whom do you review life goals and plans with? These are your allies. Many people can maintain at most eight to ten strong professional alliances at any given point in time.

The second type of relationship we'll cover is weaker ties and acquaintances. With whom are you friendly but not full-on friends? With whom do you email occasionally? Of whom can you ask a lightweight professional favor? Can you recall a conversation with this person from a couple years ago? There's quite a bit of variance in how many of these weak ties you can maintain; you may be able to maintain a maximum of a couple hundred or a couple thousand depending on your personality, your line of work, and the nature of your relationships.

Professional Allies

In 1978 twenty-year-old Mary Sue Milliken graduated from culinary school in Chicago. Despite having no real-world experience, she was determined to get a job at the best restaurant in town—the legendary Le Perroquet. After a couple weeks of lobbying, she was finally hired to peel shallots full-time. Around the same time, Susan Feniger had also just graduated from culinary school, her sights set equally high. So she moved from New York to Chicago, and months later was cleaning vegetables and steaming broccoli in the kitchen at Le Perroquet. They were the only women working in the kitchen. They were also possibly the most passionate about food—every morning they showed up to work two and a half hours before their already long and grueling shift began. They developed a friendship, but after a year or so they each wanted new professional challenges, and their paths diverged. Feniger left for Los Angeles to work at the first U.S. restaurant of the then unknown Austrian chef Wolfgang Puck. Milliken stayed in Chicago and tried to start a café of her own. When the café didn't work out, Milliken decided to improve her résumé with some experience working at restaurants in France. Though they hadn't spoken in some time, she was moved to call Feniger to say hello and pass on the news that she was soon flying across the Atlantic. Feniger's reply came as a shock: she was about to do the same. By coincidence, they were each starting new jobs in France the very next week.

Over meals at French bistros and weekend trips to small French towns, Milliken and Feniger reconnected and their relationship grew stronger, on both a personal and professional level. They dreamed of one day never having to work for someone else and perhaps even opening a restaurant of their own. When their stay in France drew to a close, they shook hands and promised each other they would work together at some point in their lives. Alas, it was not to be—at least not yet. Milliken eventually returned to Chicago and Feniger went back to Los Angeles, each picking up jobs at local restaurants.

In the months that followed, Feniger didn't let either of them forget about their pact. She urged Milliken to move to Los Angeles so they could fulfill their vision. Milliken finally did, and they launched their first venture together: City Café, a cozy café in the eastern part of the city. The two of them manned the kitchen, and a dishwasher-cum-busboy handled the dishes. Due to the limited space, they set up their grill in the parking lot behind the restaurant. It was a makeshift operation, but by its third year, lines of hungry patrons were stretching around the block. Their next restaurant was bigger and better. They called it Ciudad and specialized in Latin American cuisine. It opened to critical acclaim. The media started showing interest in this chatty, charismatic duo. The story of their years-long alliance and simultaneous ascent from the kitchen to restaurant owners and chefs was compelling, and the popularity of their restaurants in Los Angeles (and Las Vegas) spoke for itself. The Food Network gave them a TV show called *Too Hot Tamales*. Publishers courted them to write cookbooks. Three decades after meeting in that first kitchen washing food and cleaning plates, Milliken and Feniger have cemented their place as leading authorities on Latin American cuisine in the United States.

Reflecting on why their alliance has thrived, Milliken points to their complementary strengths and interests: "[F]rom the first time we got in the kitchen together, we gravitated to different sides. [Feniger] loves chaos—when there's a huge mess, and the waiters are screaming, and the cooks don't know what to do, and everybody's in a big horrible kind of catastrophe mode. That's when [Feniger] is the happiest, in the middle of that. I'm about precision and planning and not being caught in that."

Today, the alliance is evolving again. Feniger recently launched her first restaurant on her own, without Milliken as business partner. In some sense, this makes Feniger's solo restaurant a competitor to their joint operations. The two of them insist they are still strong allies. And they are. Since allies often play in the same space, sometimes they end up competing against each other. "Competitive ally" may seem like an oxymoron. But you know it's a strong alliance if you are able to navigate the occasional tricky situation with mutual respect intact.*

What are the general characteristics that make their relationship an alliance and that define your own? First, an ally is someone you consult regularly for advice. You trust his or her judgment. Second, you *proactively* share and collaborate on opportunities together. You keep your antennae especially attuned to an ally's interests, and when it makes sense to pursue something jointly, you do so. Third, you talk up an ally to other friends. You promote his or her brand. When an ally comes into conflict, you defend him, and stand up for his reputation. And he does the same for you when times get tough. There's no such thing as a fair-weather alliance; if the

---

* Milliken and Feniger were featured in Michael Eisner's thoughtful book *Working Together* (HarperBusiness, 2010), from which their story was drawn.

relationship isn't load-bearing under stress, it's not an alliance. Finally, you are explicit about your bond: "Hey, we're allies, right? How can we best help each other?"

Ron Howard and Brian Grazer, top producers and directors in Hollywood, have a legendary alliance and partnership. The essence of their alliance was well summed up by Howard: "In a business that is so crazy, to actually know that there is somebody who is really smart, who you care about, who has your interests, and who is rowing in the same direction, is something of immense value." That's an ally.

I first met Mark Pincus while at PayPal in 2002. I was giving him advice on a start-up he was working on, as my PayPal experiences were relevant. From our first conversation, I felt inspired by Mark's wild creativity and how at times he seems to bounce off the walls with energy. I'm more restrained in comparison, preferring to fit ideas into strategic frameworks instead of unleashing them fire-hose-style. Our different styles make conversation fun. But it's our similar interests and vision that have made our collaborations so successful. We invested in Friendster together in 2002, at the dawn of social networking. In 2003 the two of us bought the Six Degrees patent, which covers some of the foundational technology of social networking. Mark then started his own social network, Tribe; I started LinkedIn. When Peter Thiel and I were set to put the first money into Facebook in 2004, I suggested that Mark take half of my investment allocation. As a matter of course, I wanted to involve Mark in any opportunity that seemed intriguing, especially one that played to his social networking background—it's what you do in an alliance. In 2007, Mark called me to talk about his idea for Zynga, the social gaming company he cofounded and now leads. I knew almost immediately that I wanted to invest and join the board, which I did. Both of us thought Zynga and Facebook would be very strong companies, but no one could have predicted the astronomical heights of success. With an ally, you don't keep score, you just try to invest in the alliance as much as possible. What sustains all this collaboration? We are both driven by a passion for the Internet industry, especially the social networking space. We complement each other. We like each other as friends. We've known each other for a while—it was several years before we thought of each other as allies. And there's another seemingly insignificant reason, but it's important and worth noting: we both live in the San Francisco Bay Area. Physical proximity is actually one of the best predictors of the strength of a relationship, many studies show.

Exciting as the business outcomes have been for Mark and me, an alliance can be enriching even if lots of money is not at stake. Early in your career, allies help with self-discovery, building your network, and planning for the future. Ben's alliance with entrepreneurs Ramit Sethi and Chris Yeh is a trust bank that's primarily about deepening their shared understanding of the world. One twenty-first-century-only quality of their alliance is how they engage with one another online. Using the bookmarking service Delicious, Ramit, Chris, and Ben have been following and reading one another's favorite articles, videos, blog posts, and other Web pages for almost five years. Seeing what someone's reading is like seeing the first derivative of their thinking. Thousands of bookmarks, tweets, and blog posts later, each of them possesses an intricate understanding of what's on the others' minds on a daily basis. This means every phone call and meeting feels like it's picking up the conversation right where they left off—a few minutes ago. It comes as no surprise that when brains are so connected, trust, friendship, and fruitful business collaborations result.

An alliance is always an exchange, but not a transactional one. A transactional relationship is when your accountant files your tax returns and in exchange you pay him for his time. An alliance is when a coworker needs last-minute help on Sunday night preparing for a Monday morning presentation, and even though you're busy, you agree to go over to his house and help.

These "volleys of communication and cooperation" build trust. Trust, writes David Brooks, is "habitual reciprocity that becomes coated by emotion. It grows when two people . . . slowly learn they can rely upon each other. Soon members of a trusting relationship become willing to not only cooperate with each other but sacrifice for each other."[9]

You cooperate and sacrifice because you want to help a friend in need but also because you figure you'll be able to call on him in the future when you are the one in a bind. This isn't being selfish, it's being human. Social animals do good deeds for one another in part because the deeds will be reciprocated at some point in time. With trusted professional allies, the reciprocation isn't immediate—i.e., you don't turn around the next day and say, "Hey, I helped you with your presentation, now I want something back." Ideally, the notion of an exchange dissolves into the reality that you have intermingled fates. *In other words, as the score keeping becomes less and less formal and as the expectation for reciprocal exchange stretches over a longer and longer period of time, a relationship goes from being an exchange partnership to being a true alliance.*[*]

Weak Ties and Acquaintances: Expand the Breadth of Your Network

Allies, by the nature of the bond, are few in number. There are many more looser connections and acquaintances who also play a role in your professional life. These are folks you meet at conferences, old classmates, coworkers in other divisions, or just interesting people with interesting ideas who you come upon in day-to-day life. Sociologists refer to these contacts as "weak ties": people with whom you have spent low amounts of low-intensity time (for example, someone you might only see once or twice a year at a conference, or only know online and not in person) but with whom you're still friendly.

Weak ties in a career context were formally researched in 1973, when sociologist Mark Granovetter asked a random sample of Boston professionals who had just switched jobs how they found their new job. Of those who said they found their job through a contact, Granovetter then asked how frequently they saw the contact. He asked participants to mark whether they saw the person often (twice a week), occasionally

---

[*] Check out startupofyou.com/alliance for a lengthier explanation of altruism and reciprocity.

(more than once a year but less than twice a week), or rarely (once a year or less).[10] About 16 percent of the recipients said they found their job through a contact they saw often. The rest found their job through a contact they saw occasionally (55 percent) or rarely (27 percent). In other words, the contacts who referred jobs were "weak ties."[11] He summed up his conclusion in a paper appropriately called "The Strength of Weak Ties": The friends you don't know very well are the ones who refer winning jobs.

Granovetter accounts for this result by explaining that social cliques, which are groups of people who have something in common, often limit your exposure to wildly new experiences, opportunities, and information. Because people tend to hang out in cliques, your good friends are usually from the same industry, neighborhood, religious group, and the like. The stronger your tie with someone, the more likely they are to mirror you in various ways, and the more likely you are to want to introduce them to your other friends.[12]

From an emotional standpoint, this is great. It's fun to do things in groups with people with whom you have a lot in common. But from an informational standpoint, Granovetter argues that this interconnectedness is limiting because the same information recycles through your local network of like-minded friends. If a close friend knows about a job opportunity, you probably already know about it. Strong ties usually introduce redundancy in knowledge and activities and friend sets.

In contrast, weak ties usually sit outside of the inner circle. You're not necessarily going to introduce a looser connection to all of your other friends. Thus, there's a greater likelihood a weak tie will be exposed to new information or a job opportunity. This is the crux of Granovetter's argument: Weak ties can uniquely serve as bridges to other worlds and thus can pass on information or opportunities you have not heard about. We would stress that it's not that weak ties per se find you jobs; it's that weak ties are likely to be exposed to information or job listings you haven't seen. Weak ties in and of themselves are not especially valuable; *what is valuable is the breadth and reach of your network*.

This complicating qualification has gotten lost ever since Malcolm Gladwell touted Granovetter's study in his mega-bestseller *The Tipping Point*. Weak ties are indeed important, but they are only valuable so long as they offer new information and opportunities. Not all weak ties do. A weak tie who works in your field and is exposed to the same people and information is not going to be the bridge that Granovetter talks about. And since information is today more accessible than ever before, the bridge described by Granovetter in the 1970s is less important now than it was then. If you wanted to stay abreast of what was happening in Brazil back then, your best and perhaps only bet was to maintain a connection with someone who lived in Brazil or traveled there frequently. Now, of course, there are thousands of media sources a click away that offer insight on what's happening in distant lands. In the 1970s, if you wanted to get a job in another city, a friend in that city would have to see a job listing in the local newspaper for a local company, then snail-mail you the clipping. Today all jobs are posted online. It's easier to come by information swirling about in other social scenes, even if you don't have a weak tie yourself on the ground there. So weak ties are one way to achieve a wide-reaching network, but *any* relationship that bridges you to another world will do.*

Whichever way you introduce diversity and breadth, it's especially important during career transitions. When you pivot to Plan B or Plan Z, you'll want information about new opportunities. You'll also want to know people in different niches or fields who will encourage your move. As Herminia Ibarra says in her book *Working Identity*, sometimes it's the strong ties who know us best who may *wish* to be supportive of a transition but instead "tend to reinforce or even desperately try to preserve the old identities we are seeking to shed. Diversity and breadth in your network encourages flexibility to pivot."[13]

How Many Allies and Weak Connections Can You Have?

Imagine you receive a digital camera with a built-in memory card for your birthday. You bring it on a six-month trip to Africa where you won't have access to a computer—so all the photos you want to keep must fit on that one memory card. When you first arrive you snap photos freely, and maybe even record some short videos. But after a month or so, the memory card starts filling up. Now you're forced to be more judicious

---

* A "quasi-strong" tie, who is both different from you yet also close enough so as to make introductions, is more valuable than a weak tie, and uniquely expands the total breadth of your network. We discuss these types of connections more on www.startupofyou.com.

in deciding how to use that storage. You might take fewer pictures. You might decide to reduce the quality/resolution of the photos you do take in order to fit more. You'll probably cut back on videos. Still, inevitably, you'll hit capacity, at which point if you wish to take new photos you'll have to delete old ones. Just as a digital camera cannot store an infinite number of photos and videos, you cannot maintain an infinite number of relationships. Which is why, even if you are judicious about your choices, at some point you hit a limit, and any new relationship means sacrificing an old one.

The maximum number of relationships we can realistically manage—the number that can fit on the memory card, as it were—is described as Dunbar's Number, after evolutionary psychologist Robin Dunbar. But maybe it shouldn't be. In the early nineties, Dunbar studied the social connections within groups of monkeys and apes. He theorized that the maximum size of their overall social group was limited by the small size of their neocortex. It requires brainpower to socialize with other animals, so it follows that the smaller the primate's brain, the less efficient it is at socializing, and the fewer other primates it can befriend. He then extrapolated that humans have an especially large neocortex and so should be able to more efficiently socialize with a great number of humans. Based on our neocortex size, Dunbar calculated that humans should be able to maintain relationships with no more than roughly 150 people at a time. To cross-check the theory, he studied anthropological field reports and other clues from villages and tribes in the hunter-gatherer era. Sure enough, he found the size of surviving tribes tended to be about 150. And when he observed modern human societies, he found that many businesses and military groups organize their people into cliques of about 150. To wit: Dunbar's Number of 150.[14]

But Dunbar's research is not exactly about the total number of people that any one person can know. The research focused on how many nonhuman primates (and humans, but only by extrapolation) can survive together in a tribe. Of course, group limits and the number of people you can know are closely related concepts, especially if you consider everyone in your life to be part of your social group. Yet most of us define our total social group more broadly than Dunbar did in his research. *Survival* in the modern world doesn't depend on having direct, face-to-face contact with everyone in our social network/group, as it did for the tribes he studied.

Regardless of how you parse Dunbar's research, what is definitely the case is that there is a limit to the number of relationships you can maintain, if for no other reason than the fact that we have only twenty-four hours in each day. But, contrary to popular understanding of Dunbar's Number, there is not one blunt limit. There are different limits for each type of relationship. Think back to the digital camera. You can either take low-resolution photographs and store one hundred photos in total, or you can take high-resolution photographs and store forty. With relationships, while you can only have a few close buddies you see every day, you can stay in touch with many distant friends if you only email them once or twice a year.

But there's a twist. While the number of close allies and weak ties you can keep up is limited, those aren't your only connections. You can actually maintain a much broader social network that exceeds the size of the memory card. It's by smartly leveraging this extended network that you fully experience the power of I^{We}.

Your Extended Social Network: Second- and Third-Degree Connections

Your allies, weak ties, and the other people you know right now are your first-degree connections. À la Dunbar, there are limits to the number of first-degree connections you can have at any one time. But your friends know people you don't know. These friends of friends are your second-degree connections. And those friends of friends have friends of their own—those friends of friends of friends are your third-degree connections.

Social network theorists use degree-of-separation terminology to refer to individuals who sit within your social network. A network is a system of interconnected things, like the world's airports or the Internet (a network of computers and servers). A social network is a set of people and the connections that link them. Everyone you interact with in a professional context comprises your professional social network.

Your Network Is Bigger and More Powerful Than You Think

Think of the times you've met someone and discovered you know people in common. The clerk at the local hardware store once hiked through Yosemite with your brother-in-law. Your new girlfriend is in the same bowling league as your boss. "It's a small world," we say after such realizations. It's fun to make these unexpected connections. A busy city street can seem awash with strangers, so when we encounter a familiar face, we notice it.

But is the world actually that small? Psychologist Stanley Milgram and his student Jeffrey Travers found that it is. In fact, it's smaller and more interconnected than the occasional surprising mutual acquaintance might suggest.[15] In 1967 they conducted a famous study in which they asked a couple hundred people in Nebraska to mail a letter to someone they knew personally who might in turn know a target stockbroker in Massachusetts. Travers and Milgram tracked how long it took for the letter to pass hands and reach its destination. On average, it took six different stops before it showed up at the stockbroker's home or office in Massachusetts. In other words, the original sender in Nebraska sat six degrees apart from the recipient in Massachusetts. It was this study that birthed the Six Degrees of Separation theory, and the credible idea that you share mutual acquaintances with complete strangers on the other side of the world.

In 2001, sociologist Duncan Watts, inspired by Milgram's findings, led a more ambitious, rigorous study on a global scale.[16] He recruited eighteen targets in thirteen countries. From an archival inspector in Estonia to a policeman in Western Australia to a professor in upstate New York, the targets were selected to be as diverse as possible. Then he signed up more than sixty thousand people from across the United

States to participate in the test. They were to forward an email message to one of the eighteen targets, or to a friend who might know one of the targets. Amazingly, factoring in the emails that never made it to their destination, Watts found that Milgram had been right all along: the median distance that separated a participant from a target was between five and seven degrees.

It *is* a small world, after all. Small because it is so interconnected.

●   ●   ●

Milgram's and Watts's research shows planet Earth as one massive social network, with every human being connected to every other via no more than about six intermediary people. It's neat to ponder being connected to billions of people through your friends, and the practical implications for the start-up of you are significant as well. Suppose you want to become a doctor and would like to meet a premier M.D. in your specific field of interest. You've heard that getting an introduction is the only way you'll be able to meet her. The good news is that you know that you are at most only six degrees away from her. The bad news is that following Milgram's or Watts's procedure—asking one good friend to forward an email and hope that six or seven email forwards later the email will arrive at the target's computer—is neither efficient nor reliable. Even if it does arrive, the introduction would be highly diluted. Saying you're a friend of a friend of a friend of a friend of a friend of a friend doesn't quite carry enough heft to open doors.

But if there were a master chart of the entire human social network, you could locate the shortest possible path from you to the doctor. Now, increasingly, there is. Online social networks are converting the abstract idea of worldwide interconnectedness into something tangible and searchable. Out of an estimated one billion professionals in the world, well over 100 million of them are on LinkedIn, with more than two new members joining every second. Now, you can search this network to find the connections and friends of connections who can introduce you to that all-star doctor with the fewest number of handoffs. You don't need to randomly forward an email and hope it arrives at your destination after six twists and turns. For example, this screenshot from LinkedIn shows the intermediate hops from one user to Dr. Sarah Pendrell.

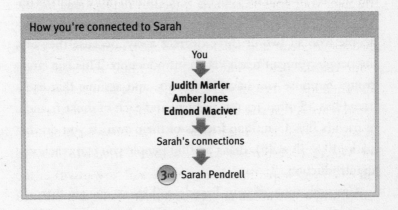

Here's where the caveat to the Six Degrees of Separation theory comes in. Academically, the theory is correct, but when it comes to meeting people who can help you professionally, *three degrees of separation* is what matters. Three degrees is the magic number because when you're introduced to a second- or third-degree connection, at least one person in an introduction chain personally knows the origin or target person. In this example: You—> Karen—> Jane—> Sarah. Karen and Jane are in the middle, and both of them know either You or Sarah—the two people who are trying to connect. That's how trust is preserved. If one additional degree of separation is added, a person in the middle of the chain will know neither You nor Sarah, and thus have no stake in making sure the introduction goes smoothly. After all, why would a person bother to introduce a total stranger (even if that stranger is a friend of a friend of a friend) to another total stranger?

So, the extended network that's available to you professionally doesn't contain the roughly seven billion other humans on the planet who sit six degrees away. But it does contain all the people who sit two or three degrees away, because they are the people you can reach via an introduction. This is a large group. Suppose you have 40 friends, and assume that each friend has 35 other friends in turn, and each of those friends of friends has 45 unique friends of their own. If you do the math ($40 \times 35 \times 45$), that's 54,000 people you can reach via an introduction.

Granted, some of your friends will know one another, so accounting for redundancy, the total number is a bit smaller. If you look at a LinkedIn user's "Network Statistics" page, which shows the size of a member's professional network to the third degree and accounts for any redundancy, you'll see it's still a big number (see chart on the next page).

You are at the center of your network. Your connections can introduce you to 2,225,400+ professionals— here's how your network breaks down:

1	**Your connections** Your trusted friends and colleagues	**170**
2	**Two degrees away** Friends of friends: each connected to one of your connections	**26,200+**
3	**Three degrees away** Reach these users through a friend and one of their friends	**2,199,100+**
	Total users you can contact through an introduction	**2,225,400+**

A person with 170 connections on LinkedIn is actually at the center of a professional network that's more than two million people strong. Now you know why one of LinkedIn's early marketing taglines was: YOUR NETWORK IS BIGGER THAN YOU THINK. It is!

And it's more powerful than you may think, too. Frank Hannigan, a software entrepreneur in Ireland, raised more than $200,000 in funding for his company in *eight days* in 2010 by reaching out to his seven hundred first-degree connections on LinkedIn and pitching them on his business. Seventy percent of those who invested were among his first-degree connections; 30 percent were second-degree connections, that is, friends of his contacts who forwarded the initial message and brokered an introduction. This is the power of the extended network.

Reach Your Second- and Third-Degree Connections via Introductions

Now that you've found the best path to a top M.D.—or that ideal angel investor, or that hiring manager with the perfect job opening, or anyone else who can open doors for you—how do you actually reach that second- or third-degree connection?[*] The best (and sometimes only) way: via an introduction from someone you know who in turn knows the person you want to reach. When you reach out to someone via an introduction from a mutual friend, it's like having a passport at the border— you can walk right through. The interaction is immediately endowed with *trust*.

I receive about fifty entrepreneur pitches by email every day. I have never funded a company directly from a cold solicitation and my guess is I never will. When an entrepreneur comes referred by introduction, someone I trust has already vetted that entrepreneur. Working within my trusted extended network allows me to move quickly when sifting through deals.

Anytime you want to meet a new person in your extended network, ask for an introduction. People know they should do this, but most don't. It's easier to cold-call. It can be awkward to ask a favor of a friend. Indeed, just because you know someone doesn't mean they have to introduce you to one of their friends. But you do have to ask—directly and specifically—and you need to present a compelling reason why the introduction makes sense. "I'd love to meet Rebecca because she works in the technology industry." Not good enough. "I'm interested in talking to Rebecca because my company is looking to partner

---

[*] Remember there's a difference between weak-tie and second- and third-degree connections. A weak tie is someone you know presently—it's a first-degree connection. A second- or third-degree connection is someone you have no present connection to, but could access via an introduction from a friend.

with companies just like hers." Better, as the introduction appears to benefit both parties. When you reach out to someone, be clear about how you intend to help the person to whom you're being introduced—or at least how you'll ensure it's not a waste of that person's time.

Figuring out how you can help the person you want to connect with—or at least figuring out the tightest point of mutual interest—does take some legwork. OkCupid, the free online dating site, analyzed more than five hundred thousand first messages between a man or a woman and a potential suitor. They found that those that garnered the highest response rates included phrases like "You mention . . ." or "I noticed that . . ." or "I'm curious what. . . ."[17] In other words, phrases that showed that the person had carefully read the other's profile. People do this in online dating, but when it comes to professional correspondence, for whatever reason, it doesn't get done. People send out appallingly unresearched and generic requests. If you spend thirty minutes researching a person in your extended network (LinkedIn is a great place to start), and tailor your request for an introduction to something you've learned, your request will stand out. For example, "I noticed you spent a summer working at a German architecture firm. I once worked for an ad agency in Berlin and am thinking about returning—perhaps we could swap notes about business opportunities in the country?"

You can conceptualize and map your network all you want, but if you can't effectively request and broker introductions, it adds up to a lot of nothing. Take it seriously. If you are not receiving or making at least one introduction a month, you are probably not fully engaging your extended professional network.

The Best Professional Network: Cohesive and Diverse

Several years ago, sociologist Brian Uzzi did a study of why certain Broadway musicals made between 1945 and 1989 were successful (like *West Side Story* or *Bye Bye Birdie*), and why others flopped.[18] What did a winner have that the loser didn't? The explanation he arrived at had to do with the social networks of the people behind the productions. For failed productions, one of two extremes was common. The first kind of failed production was collaborations between creative artists and producers who tended to all know each other from previous gigs. When there were mostly strong ties among those orchestrating the show, the production lacked the fresh, creative insights that come from diverse experience. On the opposite extreme, the other type of failed production was one in which none of the artists had experience working together. When the group was made up of mostly weak ties, teamwork and communication and group cohesion suffered. In contrast, the social networks of the people behind successful productions had a healthy balance: some of the people involved had preexisting relationships and some didn't. There were some strong ties, some weak ties. There was some established trust among the producers, but also enough new blood in the system to generate new ideas. A key factor in the success of a musical, Uzzi concluded, is an optimal blend of cohesion and creativity (that is, strong ties and weak ties) within the social networks of the people behind the scenes.

The same dynamic is also at work in places far away from the Broadway lights. The Grameen Bank, founded by Nobel Prize winner Muhammad Yunus, is loaning small amounts of money to groups of people in the impoverished villages of rural Bangladesh. These are people who would never qualify for conventional bank loans as individuals. Yunus's pioneering insight was that loaning to groups rather than individuals creates peer pressure within the group to pay back the loans, reducing the risk of default. But Grameen doesn't loan money to just any group that walks in the door. The loan analyst looks for groups most likely to repay the loan, and one of the best predictors of that is the structure of the group's social network. Sociologists Nicholas Christakis and James Fowler summarize the bank's approach as follows: "Grameen Bank fosters strong ties within groups that optimize trust and then connects them via weaker ties to members of other groups to optimize their ability to find creative solutions when problems arise."[19] Strong connections optimize trust because there's likely overlap in belief systems and communication styles. Weak connections help find creative solutions by introducing new information and resources from other social circles.

Think of your network of relationships in the same way: The best professional network is both narrow/deep (strong connections) and wide/shallow (bridge ties).

Only strong connections provide depth, of course, which is why these more intimate alliances are the most important kind of bond. But they can also be helpful for breadth in ways weak ties cannot. Your stronger connections are more likely to happily introduce you to new people—to your second- and third-degree connections. Weak connections, while valuable sources of new information, will not usually introduce you to *other* people unless they have a compelling transactional reason (i.e., unless it benefits them in some way). Again, Granovetter would point out the redundancy problem of strong ties—most of your good friends know one another and therefore anyone they'd introduce you to would be someone you either (a) already know or (b) wouldn't obtain any new or interesting information from. Which is why you should relish opportunities to build trust connections with folks in different fields or social circles. Prize diversity, though don't resolutely seek it out in a way that can come off as calculated. When you hit it off with someone who is meaningfully different from you, know that the relationship has the potential to be both genuinely enriching as well as a way to expand the breadth of information and creativity that flows through your network.

• • •

By now you should see why there's a big difference between being the *most* connected person and being the *best* connected person.[20] The value and strength of your network are not represented in the number of contacts in your address book. What matters are your alliances, the strength and diversity of your trust connections, the freshness of the information flowing through your network, the breadth of your weak ties, and the ease with which you can reach your second- or third-degree connections. There are, in short, several factors that contribute to a fulfilling, helpful professional network.

Your approach to your network should be unique to you. When you're young and exploratory, many weaker connections in disparate fields may be especially valuable. When you're midflight, perhaps you want to shore up alliances and make deep connections in certain niche areas. Whatever your priorities, nurture the network you're building. Your professional life depends on your being smart and generous with the people you care about.

HOW TO STRENGTHEN AND MAINTAIN YOUR NETWORK

Relationships are living, breathing things. Feed, nurture, and care about them: they grow. Neglect them: they die. This goes for any type of relationship on any level of intimacy. The best way to strengthen a relationship is to jump-start the long-term process of give-and-take. Do something for another person. Help him or her. But how?

Here's a good example. When Jack Dorsey was cofounding Square—the mobile payments company that turns any smartphone into a device that accepts the swipe of a credit card—he had loads of investor interest. For killer entrepreneurs with a killer idea, it's actually the investors who compete for the privilege to invest. Digg and Milk founder Kevin Rose had seen a prototype of the Square device and immediately realized the potential for small businesses. When he asked Jack if there was room for another person to join the initial round of funding, Jack told him it was full—they didn't need more investors. That was that. But Kevin still wanted to be helpful. He noticed that Square didn't have a video demo on their website showing how the device worked. So he put together a hi-def video showing off the device and then showed the video to Jack just as an fyi. Impressed, Jack turned around and invited Kevin to invest in the "full" Series A round of financing. Kevin found a way to add value. He didn't ask for anything in return—he just made the video and showed it to Jack. No strings attached. Not surprisingly, Jack appreciated the effort and returned the favor.

Helping someone out means acknowledging that you are capable of helping. Reject the misconception that if you're less powerful, less wealthy, or less experienced, you have nothing to offer someone else. Everyone is capable of offering helpful support or constructive feedback. To be sure, you'll be *most* helpful if you have the skills and experiences to help your allies. Pleasant friendships are nice, but the best-connected professionals are ones who can really help their allies. This is what makes a professional network and not simply a social one.

Next, figure out what kind of help is helpful. Imagine sitting down to lunch with an acquaintance you just met and opening the conversation by saying, "I'm looking for a job in New York City." He puts down his fork, wipes the barbecue sauce off his face, looks you square in the eye, and replies, "I know the *perfect* job for you." Is that helpful? Hardly. Since he likely has no idea what the perfect job means to you, a better response would have probed: "Tell me more about your skills, interests, and background." Good intentions are never enough. To give helpful help you need to have a sense of your friend's values and priorities so that your offer of help can be relevant and specific. What keeps him up at 2 a.m.? What are his talents? His interests? Asking "How can I help you?!" immediately after meeting someone is overeager. First you must know the person.

Finally, once you understand his needs, challenges, and desires, think about how you can offer him a small gift. We don't mean an Amazon.com gift card or a box of cigars. We mean something—even something intangible—that costs you almost nothing yet still is valuable to the other person. Classic small gifts include relevant information and articles, introductions, and advice. A really expensive big gift is actually counterproductive—it can feel like a bribe. Inexpensive yet thoughtful is best.

When deciding what kind of gift to give, think about your unique experiences and skills. What might you have that the other person does not? For example, consider an extreme hypothetical. What kind of gift would be helpful to Bill Gates? Probably not introducing him to somebody—he can meet whomever he wants. Probably not sending an article you read in the media about the Gates Foundation—he was probably interviewed for it. Probably not by investing in one of his projects—he's doing fine money-wise. Instead, think about little things. For example, if you're in college, or have a good friend or sibling in college, you could send him information about some of the key cultural and technology-usage trends among the college set. Intel on what college students—the next generation—are thinking or doing is always of interest yet hard to get no matter how much money you have. What specific things do you know or have that the other person does not? The secret behind stellar small gifts is that it's something you can uniquely provide.

Finally, if the best way to strengthen a relationship is to help the other person, the second best way is to let yourself be helped. As Ben Franklin recommended, "If you want to make a friend, let someone do you a favor." Don't view help skeptically (What did I do to deserve this?) or with suspicion (What's the hidden agenda here?). Well, sometimes second-guessing is warranted, but not usually. People like helping. If someone offers to introduce you to a person you really want to meet or offers to share assorted wisdom on an important topic, accept the help and express due gratitude. Everyone will feel good—and you'll actually get closer to the person.

Be a Bridge

A good way to help people is to introduce them to people and experiences they wouldn't otherwise be able to access. In other words, straddle different communities/social circles and then be the bridge that your friends can walk over. My passion for entrepreneurship combined with my interest in board game design led me to introduce many of my entrepreneur friends to Settlers of Catan, the German board game. A community in Silicon Valley has sprung up around the game. I've also combined my experience scaling consumer Internet products with my interest in cause-based philanthropy to help organizations like Kiva and Mozilla—bridging my network and expertise from the for-profit world to the not-for-profit world. Ben's experiences and skills make him a bridge between his friends in California and Latin America; between businesspeople in their twenties and businesspeople much older; and between businesspeople and publishing professionals. Can you develop skill sets, interests, and experiences in two or more domains and then act as a bridge for your connections in one circle who want to access the other? If so, you will be enormously helpful.

In Touch and Top of Mind

There is nothing worse than receiving an out-of-the-blue email from someone you haven't spoken to in three years: "Hey, we met a few years ago at that conference. Listen, I'm looking for a job in the marketing world—do you know anyone hiring?" You think, Oh, I see, you only contact me when you need something.

When a busy person gets an email asking if she knows someone for an open job position or if she can recommend an expert on a certain topic, the people who come to mind will be the people with whom she's had a recent interaction. Will she think of you when that chance opportunity crosses her desk? Only if you're top of mind—only if you're at the top of her inbox or newsfeed.

It's not technically hard to stay in touch with people. Though you wouldn't know it based on how frequently you hear someone sheepishly explain months of no contact with, "Sorry, I'm really bad at keeping in touch," as if dropping someone a quick email were an innate aptitude like sense of direction. In fact, all it takes to stay in touch with the people you know is a desire to do so and a modest amount of organization and proactiveness. You've probably heard a lot of the common advice on this front. Here are some nonobvious things to keep in mind.

- *You're probably not nagging.* A common fear people have about staying in touch and following up is that the other person will perceive you as annoying and pushy. You write someone and ask if she wants to grab coffee. No response. You forward your email a week later and repeat the question. No response. Now what? Do you come off as needy if you follow up yet again? Well, it depends. But usually not. Keep following up politely if you don't get an answer—and try to mix up the message, the gift, the approach. With the amount of noise polluting people's inbox, it's common for emails to get buried. Until you hear "No," you haven't been turned down.
- *Try to add value.* Check in with someone when you can offer something more than a generic greeting or personal update. Examples: you see his name in the news, read an article

he wrote or was quoted in, or know a qualified candidate for a position he is trying to fill. It's unimpressive to send a note simply asking, "How are you?"

• *If you're worried about seeming too personal, couch your staying-in-touch as a mass action.* Does it feel weird reaching out to a high school classmate you haven't spoken to in years? Here's a tip that runs counter to the general principle of personalizing your communications: Couch your initial getting-back-in-touch action as part of a more generic process: "I'm trying to reconnect with old classmates from high school. How are you?" This reduces some of the potential awkwardness. Once you've eased back into personal contact, then personalize your message.

• *One lunch is worth dozens of emails.* A one-hour lunch with a person creates a bond that would take dozens of electronic communications. When you can, meet in person.

• *Social media.* Social media is particularly great for staying in touch passively. As you push one-to-many updates out to your network and followers, if someone you know wants to respond, he or she can. But there's no obligation. Because many people do *not* respond to every status update, tweet, or shared article, it can be easy to think no one is reading. But they are. The drip, drip, drip of short, regular updates—even if some border on the frivolous—creates real human connection between you and your online connections. Use LinkedIn to post professional updates; Facebook to post personal updates; and Twitter for updates that may appeal to both groups.

If you've fallen out of touch with someone, be the one to reconnect. Dive right back into things, perhaps with a sheepish note up-front saying that "it's been too long." Reactivating once strong relationships from school or a previous employer or previous geography is a real pleasure, and it's one of the easiest ways to build "new" meaningful connections.

Set up an "Interesting People" Fund

You might be nodding your head at the importance of staying in touch. But will you actually follow through? Enacting behavioral change isn't easy. When you actually have to *do* the thing you know is important, it's tempting to push it off for another day. That's why Steve Garrity and Paul Singh budgeted and precommitted real time and money to staying in touch—so they'd have no excuses when it came time to do so.

Steve Garrity studied computer science at Stanford and interned at start-ups over the summers. After graduating from a master's program in 2005, he was convinced he wanted to start a technology company of his own in Silicon Valley. But he had spent his entire adult life to that point in the Bay Area and was worried that if he started a company right away, he would be tied down in one location for many more years. He wanted a change of scenery first. So he took a job as an engineer at Microsoft, near Seattle, to work on their mobile search technology. Seattle was a new physical place and Microsoft was a big company—while neither the location nor the big company culture was what he planned to do long-term, he figured the new experiences would be enlightening.

But Garrity had one big worry: What would happen to his network of Silicon Valley entrepreneurs, venture capitalists, and friends? He knew he would someday move back to start a company. He did not want his local network to become stale. So he made a point to stay in touch with all of his Bay Area connections. Here's where Garrity got creative. Instead of just thinking about the importance of staying in touch (but eventually falling out of touch, which is what usually happens), he set aside time and money in advance to keep his network up-to-date. The state of Washington doesn't tax personal (or corporate) income, so Garrity figured he was saving a meaningful amount of money by living there instead of California. Upon moving to Seattle, he declared that seven thousand dollars of his savings would be "California money."

Anytime someone interesting in the Valley invited him to lunch, dinner, or coffee, Garrity promised himself he would fly to San Francisco to do the meeting. He treated the plane flight like an hour-long car ride. One of his old Stanford professors called him, not realizing Garrity had left town: "Steve, some really interesting students are coming over to my house tomorrow night. I think you'd enjoy meeting them. Want to join?" Steve said yes, and booked his flight to San Francisco. The following evening, he arrived at the professor's house and knocked on the door with one hand and held a suitcase in the other. Because he had allocated money to follow through on a predecided policy, he didn't have to worry about the cost of flights or the stress of decision making.

Over his three and a half years at Microsoft, Garrity visited the Bay Area at least once a month. It paid off. After returning to California in 2009, he started a company, Hearsay Labs, with one of his San Francisco friends—a friend whose couch served as his bed during his regular pilgrimages to the Bay Area from Seattle.

Garrity is not the only one who's figured out that precommitting yourself to do something makes sure it actually happens. Paul Singh grew up, went to college, and worked his first few jobs all in the Washington, DC, metro area. In 2007 he moved to Northern California to work at a technology company. He was concerned his East Coast connections would wither during his stint on the West Coast. So he set aside three thousand dollars a year to fly back to Washington with the purpose of spending time with his friends out there. In addition to maintaining existing relationships, Paul also used the money to meet new people. He referred to his savings allotment as the "interesting people fund"—money earmarked to stay in touch with or meet new, interesting people. After a few years in the Bay Area, Singh is back in Washington, DC, working as an entrepreneur-in-residence at a small investment fund, an opportunity that arose thanks to meeting his new boss via his interesting people fund. With a bigger bank account, Singh has upped his interesting people fund to a thousand dollars per month, and he uses it mainly to reconnect with the network he built in the Bay Area during his time there.

Navigate Status Dynamics When Dealing with Powerful People

If you want to maintain relationships with busy, powerful people, you have to pay special attention to the role of status. *Status* refers to a person's power, prestige, and rank within a given social setting at a given moment in time. There is no one pecking order in life; status is relative and dynamic. David Geffen is high status in the entertainment world, for example, but perhaps comparatively less so if Steven Spielberg is in the room. Likewise, Brad Pitt is high-status, but put him in a room full of software engineers when the project at hand involves coding, and his status is irrelevant. The President of the United States is often referred to as the most powerful man in the world, yet there are things Bill Gates can do that the president cannot, and still other things that Oprah Winfrey can do that Gates cannot. A person's status depends on the circumstances and on who's around.

You won't read about status in most business and career books. It is a topic often dodged in favor of bromides like "Treat people with respect" or "Be considerate of the other person's time." Good advice, but not the whole story. The business world is rife with power jostling, gamesmanship, and status signaling, like it or not. It's especially important to understand these dynamics when you work with people more powerful than you.

Before Robert Greene became a bestselling author, he worked for an agency in Hollywood that sold human-interest stories to magazines, film producers, and publishers. His job was to find the stories. A competitive person, Greene wanted to be the best, and sure enough, as he recalls, he was finding more stories that got turned into magazine articles, books, and movies than anyone else in his office.

One day, Greene's supervisor took him aside and told him that she wasn't very happy with him. She was not specific, but she made it clear that something just wasn't working. Greene was befuddled. He was producing lots of stories that were being sold—wasn't that the point? There was something else. He wondered if he was not communicating well. Perhaps it was just an interpersonal issue. So he focused more on engaging her, communicating, and being likeable. He met with his boss to go over his process and his thinking. But nothing changed—except for his ongoing success at finding really good stories to sell. Later, during a staff meeting, the tensions boiled over, and the supervisor interrupted the meeting and told Greene he had an attitude problem. No more detail, just that he wasn't being a good listener and had a bad attitude.

A few weeks later, after being tortured by the vague criticisms despite his solid work performance, Greene quit. A job that should have been a stellar professional success had turned into a nightmare. Over the course of the next several weeks, he reflected on what had gone wrong with his boss.

He had assumed that what mattered was doing a great job and showing everyone how talented he was. While doing a great job was certainly necessary, he concluded it was not enough. What he failed to recognize was how his personal talents might make his boss look diminished in the eyes of others. He failed to navigate the status dynamics around him; failed to account for the insecurities, status anxieties, and egos of everyone else. He failed to build relationships with the people above him and below him on the totem pole. And ultimately, he paid the price with his job.

Everyone Is Equal, and Yet Everyone Is Not Equal

All men are created equal and endowed with inalienable rights to life, liberty, and the pursuit of happiness, rights guaranteed regardless of gender, race, or religion. If a man commits a crime, he may lose his liberty but not his basic human rights such as food and humane living conditions (at least in enlightened societies, anyway). No one is more human than the next person. If you breathe, you deserve basic dignity. Period.

But in other ways, people are not equal. We do not live in an egalitarian society. People make different choices. Good luck falls on some more than others. Compare two men who work in finance, wear a suit and tie every day, and live in New York City. On the surface they may seem to be equal in status, but in reality one person will always be (and be perceived as) relatively more accomplished, powerful, rich, intelligent, busy, or famous than the other.

Status differences—both real and perceived—bear on how you are expected to act in different social situations. The following scenarios show how inappropriate power moves can offend someone of equal or higher status, and how to avoid making them.

• You email the vice president in charge of hiring at a company you want to work for. You send your résumé and propose to meet at a coffee shop near your house.

> A meeting should usually be made more convenient for the higher-status person. That means at the time and location best for him or her. When corresponding with higher-status people, propose to meet "in or near your office."

• You show up late to a meeting with a fellow product manager.

> Tardiness is the classic power move because it says, "My time is more valuable than yours, so it's okay for you to wait for me." To be sure, we've all been late due to circumstances out of our control, so it's not always a reliable signal. But usually it says something. Think about it: Would you allow yourself to be late to a meeting with Barack Obama? Certainly not.

• You and your coworker are both marketing assistants at your company. He mentions he's working on a sales proposal. You proactively say, "I'd be more than happy to take a look and tell you how it could be improved."

> Sounds harmless? Usually it is harmless. But be careful. When you make the unsolicited offer to tell someone how they can improve, you're implying that you

are able to see flaws in his work that he cannot see, and that he ought to be happy to accept your feedback. If the other person sees himself as your peer, he may not view you as someone who should be telling him how to improve, and may be resentful rather than appreciative.

Remember, even if you aren't trying to signal you are more powerful, an inadvertent power move is still a power move, and it can irritate decision makers you'd rather impress.

• • •

The conclusion is not to suck up to people of higher status. Slavishly affirming everything an important person says is unimpressive, to say nothing of dishonest. Nor is the answer to disrespect people of lower status or to flaunt superiority. Presenting yourself as a Big Deal repels people below you, who won't feel inspired or loyal. It also repels people above you, who will interpret your braggadocio as insecurity. Rather, the point is that some people require a bit more finesse. If you want to build a relationship with someone of higher status, know that you are supposed to be accommodating.

The social terrain at the highest levels of power and influence can be treacherous. If you wish to cultivate and strengthen ties with your boss, boss's boss, top officials, or other people in high places, think about how the power imbalance affects your expected social behavior. A little bit of conscientiousness in this department goes a long way.

When to Let Go

People change. You change. Some relationships just aren't meant to last beyond a certain point. Unfortunately, it's sometimes easier to let the relationship continue out of inertia unless there's a strong catalyst to change, which means some people keep up friendships that should really be retired.

Millennials are particularly prone to this bias. In college you're placed in close proximity with other age-similar peers and together you rack up a tremendous number of shared experiences. It's easy to have a conversation over dinner about what so-and-so said at last night's party in the dorms. But in the real world you aren't living every second together, so those friendships now depend on genuine shared passions and values. At the same time, your interests and attitudes evolve. One of the best things about adulthood is that you meet people who share your specific interests and intellectual verve. Often what you end up with is a situation where your school or childhood friends are part of an important emotional history, but some of them do not seem as interesting as newer friends you are meeting. What to do?

Certainly you should do something, because you won't have the time or energy to cultivate new friendships if you relentlessly hold on to old ones. It's that digital camera again: you won't have the space on your hard drive. But unlike with a digital camera, the right move isn't to actively "delete" friendships you wish not to keep up. Rather, it's okay to simply let those friendships fade. This is a natural evolution of some relationships. Unlike romantic relationships, with friendships there's rarely a reason to have a full-on breakup. Even if people go in different directions and the friendship slowly peters out, trust can endure. And unlike most exes, it is possible to re-kindle/reactivate friendships later on when your lives are more aligned.

Many relationships fade unknowingly and unfortunately. Actively maintain the relationships you value, and consciously let fade those you do not.

INVEST IN YOURSELF

In the next day:

- Look at your calendar for the past six months and identify the five people you spend the most time with—are you happy with the influence those five people are having on you?

In the next week:

- Introduce two people you know who do not know each other. Make sure the intro will be useful to both sides. (Visit startupofyou.com if you need help on how to craft the actual introduction email.) Then think about a challenge you are dealing with and ask an existing connection for an introduction to someone who could help. Jump-start the process by offering a small gift (such as a relevant article) to the person you want to meet.

- Imagine you got laid off from your job today. Who are the ten people you'd email to solicit their advice on what to do next? Reach out to them now, when you don't need anything specifically.

In the next month:

- Pick one person in your network who is a weaker tie but with whom you might like to have a stronger alliance. Commit to trying to help him or her proactively by giving small gifts. These can be anything from sending the person an interesting article to helping them prepare for a presentation to forwarding a job posting. Invest serious time and energy in the relationship over several months.

- Create an "interesting people fund" to which you automatically funnel a certain percentage of your paycheck. Use it to pay for coffees, lunches, and the occasional plane ticket to meet new people and shore up existing relationships.

Network Intelligence

It's not just the people you know. It's the people *they* know—your second- and third-degree connections. Plan an event where your friends bring a few of *their* friends; invite your extended network.

More advanced tips on how to invest in your network are available at www.startupofyou.com.

5
Pursue Breakout Opportunities

Success begins with opportunities. Opportunities are like the snap to the quarterback in football. You still have to move the ball down the field; you still have to execute. But without a snap to the quarterback, there's no touchdown. For a young lawyer, an opportunity could mean being assigned to work with the smartest partner in the firm. For an artist, it could be a last-minute offer (perhaps due to a cancellation) to exhibit at a prominent museum. For a student, it could mean being awarded a rare scholarship to travel and do research.

If finding these opportunities were a matter of simply walking into a store, rifling through a dusty bin of opportunities, picking one, and then checking out, the hierarchy of power in the world would look quite a bit different. Of course, it doesn't work that way. It's up to you—with the help of your network—to go out and find and develop professional opportunities for yourself. And not just any old opportunity will do. Entrepreneurs don't start businesses just anywhere; they channel the mind-set and skills we've been discussing into finding the *great* business opportunities. Likewise, in order to accomplish something significant in your career, you need to focus on finding and capitalizing on those *great* career opportunities: the opportunities that will extend your competitive advantage and accelerate your Plan A or Plan B.

In a start-up, growth usually isn't slow and steady. Instead, unusually consequential opportunities—certain breakthroughs, deals, discoveries—rocket the company forward and accelerate the rate of growth. Look at Groupon. For the first year or so of its existence it hobbled along as a site you've probably never heard of called The Point, which organized groups of people who wanted to pledge unified support for social and civic causes. Andrew Mason, the site's proprietor, noticed the site's users were most engaged when they banded together to increase their buying power. He saw this as an opportunity to break into a different niche. So he pivoted to a new plan and built a site (in a matter of weeks) that exclusively offered group discounts to consumers. Thanks to his fast action and superb execution, this move massively accelerated the growth trajectory of the company, eventually transforming The Point into Groupon and the multibillion-dollar public company it is today. But no start-up enjoys astronomical growth forever—at least not without continuing to find new breakthrough opportunities. As Groupon's growth has been challenged by competition, Andrew and his teammates are looking for new opportunities. A promising one is mobile, location-based deals for consumers on the go. This venture, Groupon Now, allows retailers with perishable inventory (such as restaurants) to bring customers into their stores at otherwise unpopular hours. If it succeeds, it will set in motion another huge acceleration in growth. Groupon's trajectory, in other words, looks more like the "reality" graph below.

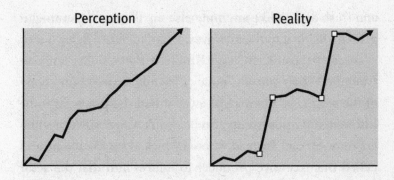

Perception   Reality

Careers, like start-ups, are also punctuated with breakouts. On a typical résumé—and even on a LinkedIn profile—there's a reverse chronological listing of jobs held, all presented in the same type size and font. But on its face this is misleading. Our professional lives are not a sequence of equally important jobs. There are always *breakout* projects, connections, specific experiences, and yes, strokes of luck—that lead to unusually rapid career growth.

Consider the famous career of George Clooney. In 1982, the young man from Kentucky moved to Hollywood, like so many before him, with a dream of becoming a movie star. He had a few things in his favor: good looks, some natural talent, a strong work ethic, and a couple family connections. Yet after twelve years of auditioning he had only landed occasional appearances on B-list television shows. Clooney was a long way from motion pictures. That all changed in 1994, when he caught wind of an opportunity, hustled to seize it, and catapulted his career to new heights.

Warner Bros. was producing an expensive, fast-paced, gritty medical drama called *ER*, with "a script so exciting and fresh and unlike anything else on TV that, assuming it actually made it to the airwaves, it had to either flame out or succeed spectacularly," says Kimberly Potts, in her book on Clooney. When one of Clooney's friends showed him a copy of the script, he knew right away it had the potential to be his breakout opportunity. So he didn't wait for *ER* producers to reach out. Instead, Clooney picked up the phone and called the executive producer to inform him that the actor wasn't going to let anyone else get the lead doctor role. They invited him to audition. He soon got a call-back with good news. "I just got a career," Clooney said to a friend, after hanging up the phone. Indeed, "his career, his entire life and the lives of those around him were about to take off on a whole new trajectory."[1] The show was a huge hit. Riding its success, he left television and pursued his dream of being on the big screen. After a few so-so movies, he landed a leading role in the movie *Out of Sight* and then the blockbuster film *Ocean's Eleven*, the first of a highly successful trilogy. And he was soon among the leading stars in Hollywood—in a fraction of the time it had taken him to land that game-changing role on *ER*.

So how did Clooney recognize the *ER* role for the breakout opportunity that it was? Well, he was not certain it would be a breakout. You can never be certain. Golden opportunities are not wrapped in pretty packaging with a clear label; killer job opportunities are rarely advertised on job boards. But *ER* had some telling characteristics, and he picked up on them. One key fact was that the other people involved in the show were high quality—always important. Another was that Clooney hadn't yet played the lead role on a major network drama.

It would be a challenge. A career move that makes you feel in over your head stretches you in new dimensions and usually contains significant upside.

It may be tempting to dismiss Clooney's breakout opportunity as only good luck. Was Clooney simply in the right place at the right time? Yes, and there is an element of luck to that. *But you can develop habits of behavior and habits of thinking that increase the likelihood that you find yourself in the right place at the right time.* You can, in other words, deliberately increase the quality and quantity of career opportunities— even if you don't know what and where they are just yet.

MIND ON FIRE: BE CURIOUS

There's one disposition and mind-set that must be "on" like electricity to power all the other opportunity-seeking behaviors: curiosity. Entrepreneurs brim with curiosity: they see opportunity where others see problems, because while others simply complain, entrepreneurs ask *Why*? Why the heck doesn't this annoying product/service work as well as it should? Is there a better way? And can I make money off it? Andrew Mason's idea for The Point came to him that way: he was trying to cancel a cell phone contract, and it was such a hassle that he wondered if the collective pressure of multiple unhappy customers would force the company to be more efficient. You could even say that entrepreneurship begins in frustrated wonderment! For entrepreneurs this mix translates into supreme alertness for new business opportunities. For you in your career, curiosity (with or without frustration) about industries, people, and jobs will make you alert to professional opportunities. It's hard to learn curiosity. But it's something you can get infected with by hanging out with passionately curious people. And once you catch curiosity, it's (luckily) hard to shake.

When your eyes are open and your mind is curious, you can do things that dramatically increase your opportunity flow, such as tap networks of people, court selective randomness, and see opportunity amid hardship. In this chapter we'll explore each of these concepts and how they can be valuable to your career. But don't expect an immediate return. Andrew Mason did not wake up one day and conceive Groupon; the opportunity grew out of his ongoing activities and ideas. Clooney did not move to Hollywood and the next day land the *ER* gig. He invested twelve years of continuous effort. To cultivate, identify, and generate an opportunity takes ongoing investment.

So even if you don't have an immediate reason to actively look for an explicit opportunity—even if, say, you're happily employed and stimulated—it's important to keep generating professional opportunities anyway. Partly this builds opportunity muscle memory: the more you try, the more you strengthen your intuitive sense of how, where, and why opportunities enter your career. Partly it's because you never know when you'll have to pivot to Plan B and go after a new opportunity. LinkedIn surfaces job recommendations automatically based on your profile content, location, and attributes of people like you—and it will display these jobs to you even if you haven't indicated you are looking for a job. It was functionality inspired by a recruiter who said, "Everyone's looking for an opportunity, even if they don't know it."

HOW TO FIND AND GENERATE CAREER OPPORTUNITIES

Court Serendipity and Good Randomness

In the chapter on planning and adapting, we saw how the stories of both winning start-ups and notable careers rarely fit into a tidy, linear narrative—that despite the common assumption that entrepreneurs (or professionals) craft a single plan for their company (or career), then work tirelessly and single-mindedly to bring that plan to fruition, most successful companies and careers in fact go through many adaptations and iterations. They never really arrive at a fixed destination; it's an endless journey. Along these lines, it's easy in hindsight to attribute breakthrough career opportunities to a master plan. "And then, since I knew Nancy would be crucial to my success, I decided to randomly bump into her at a party. . . ." Yeah, right. What more often happens is that you stumble upon the person or idea without specifically intending to. The key, then, is to raise the likelihood that you stumble upon something valuable—namely, by courting good randomness and seeing the opportunities that reveal themselves.

For John D'Agostino it all started because of a chance encounter in September 2002 at the Waldorf-Astoria hotel in New York City. D'Agostino was attending an event hosted by the Italian American Foundation to honor Vincent Viola, the chairman of the New York Mercantile Exchange (NYMEX). The NYMEX is where futures contracts for energy products (mainly oil) are bought and sold. Billions of dollars of transactions make it the world's largest physical commodities futures exchange—and it made Vincent Viola a very powerful man indeed. D'Agostino, then in his twenties, was at the dinner to thank the foundation for helping pay for his business school tuition. His brief remarks caught the attention of Viola. Afterward, Viola handed D'Agostino his business card and said, "See if you can get on my calendar." D'Agostino, an aspiring mogul, felt as a wannabe rock star would if Bono offered to give a few music lessons for free. He knew this was an opportunity he could not let pass. He fastidiously followed up and, after a dozen calls to Viola's secretary, finally secured a dinner date. He got hired as a manager for special projects at the NYMEX, where he laid the groundwork for a joint energy exchange with the Dubai Development and Investment Authority. He was eventually promoted to vice president of strategy at the NYMEX (and was the subject of a book subtitled *The True Story of an Ivy League Kid Who Changed the World of Oil, from Wall Street to Dubai*). Not bad for a chance encounter.

Serendipity is the delightful word we use to describe accidental good fortune. An English novelist named Horace Walpole coined the word to describe a phenomenon he first observed in an old Persian fairy tale called "The Three Princes of Serendip." In the story, the king sends his three sons on a journey to distant lands. The princes come upon some problems; at one point they are accused of thievery. Yet they exercise such impeccable judgment and insight (when exonerating themselves from charges that they stole a camel) that their father and other rulers decide to grant them the opportunity to become rulers and kings themselves. In a letter to a friend, Walpole says "serendipitous" is how he refers to the accidental good fortune of the Serendip princes: they got lucky, to be sure, but they also acted sagely and wisely in turning unexpected setbacks into opportunities. Winning the lottery is blind luck. Serendipity involves being alert to potential opportunity and acting on it.

Still, even if you are curious and alert, opportunities won't just fall into your lap. Almost every case of serendipity and opportunity involves someone doing something. D'Agostino was attending an event and making himself available and responsive to the powerful people he met. Clooney was out auditioning for roles. Andrew Mason at Groupon was iterating on a website. In the Persian fairy tale, the Princes of Serendip "were not simply dallying their lives away in luxury in Sri Lanka on some convenient palace couch. They were out on the move, exploring, traveling widely when they encountered their accidental good fortune," says James Austin in his book *Chase, Chance, and Creativity*.[2] There's a reason the story that inspired the word *serendipity* involves exploration and journeys. You won't encounter accidental good fortune—you won't stumble upon opportunities that rocket your career forward—if you're lying in bed. When you *do something*, you stir the pot and introduce the possibility that seemingly random ideas, people, and places will collide and form new combinations and opportunities.[3] By being in motion, you are spinning a web as wide and as tall as possible in order to catch any interesting opportunities that come your way.

It's easy to say you should be in motion—but move where, specifically? We'll suggest some specific action items at the end of the chapter, but courting randomness can be as simple as extending your next trip to a different city by a day and meeting up with friends of friends. Or going to a dinner party where you don't know anyone. Or picking up a magazine you don't normally read.

Obviously, motion in literally *any* direction is unwise. Backpacking around Darfur, for example, would generate randomness of the wrong sort. But if the goal is to court good randomness, you don't want to be too *directed* in your motion, either. Most of the time you simply do not know when, where, and how opportunity will knock. At which conference will you fortuitously bump into the friend of your mother who's hiring in his medical office this summer? Which producer in Hollywood will return your nth voicemail and request a copy of your screenplay? Might a big-name reporter start following you on Twitter and start calling you for quotes? There's no way of knowing for sure. So be open-minded, but set smart parameters. You can go to a conference and approach random people; but better yet, you can go to a conference, identify someone you know is interesting, and approach the people you see that interesting person talking to. You're courting randomness, but you're also being strategic.

As always, be yourself above all. Do the things that you think you will benefit from—the things that play off your competitive advantage and each of the three puzzle pieces. Going to parties is an obvious way to put yourself out there, but if you don't like parties, don't go to them.

As entrepreneur Bo Peabody says, "The best way to ensure that lucky things happen is to make sure a lot of things happen."[4] Make things happen, and in the long run, you'll design your own serendipity, and make your own opportunities.

Connect to Human Networks: Groups and Associations of People

Opportunities do not float like clouds. They are firmly attached to individuals. If you're looking for an opportunity, you're really looking for *people*. If you're evaluating an opportunity, you're really evaluating *people*. If you're trying to marshal resources to go after an opportunity, you're really trying to enlist the support and involvement of other *people*. A company doesn't offer you a job, *people* do.

In the previous chapter we discussed how to build a network of professional alliances and weaker, bridge ties. Here we want to explore how opportunities flow through congregations of these people. Those with good ideas and information tend to hang out with one another. You will get ahead if you can tap the circles that dish the best opportunities. It's how people have gotten ahead for centuries.

Roll the clock back more than two hundred years. In 1765 Joseph Priestley, a young amateur scientist and minister, was running experiments in his makeshift laboratory in the

English countryside. He was exceptionally bright but isolated from any peers, until one December day when he traveled into London to attend the Club of Honest Whigs. The brainchild of Benjamin Franklin, the club was like an eighteenth-century version of the networking groups that exist today. Franklin, who was in England promoting the interests of the American colonies, convened his big-thinking friends at the London Coffee House on alternating Thursdays. Their conversations on science, theology, politics, and other topics of the day were freewheeling and reflected the coffeehouse setting. Priestley attended to get feedback on a book idea about scientists' progress on understanding electricity. He got much more than feedback. Franklin and his friends swelled in support of Priestley: they offered to open their private scientific libraries to him. They offered to review drafts of his manuscript. They offered their friendship and encouragement. Crucially, Priestley reciprocated all the way: he was committed to circulating his ideas and discoveries through his social network, thereby strengthening the interpersonal bonds, refining the ideas themselves, and increasing the likelihood that his new connections would help him exploit whatever opportunities were found. In short, Priestley's night at the coffeehouse dramatically altered the trajectory of his career (much like Clooney's *ER* role did). According to author Steven Johnson in his book *The Invention of Air*, Priestley went from semi-isolation to plugging into "an existing network of relationships and collaborations that the coffeehouse environment facilitated."[5] He went on to have an illustrious scientific and writing career, famously discovering the existence of oxygen. The London

Coffee House went on to become "a central hub of innovation in British society."[6]

It wasn't Franklin's first time rounding up friends for regular discussion. Forty years earlier, he had convinced twelve of his "most ingenious" friends (as he referred to them in his autobiography) in Philadelphia to form a club dedicated to mutual improvement. Meeting one night a week, these young men recommended books, ideas, and contacts to one another. They fostered self-improvement through discussions on philosophy, morals, economics, and politics. They called the club the Junto ("hoon-toe"). The Junto became a private forum for brainstorming and a surreptitious instrument for leading public opinion. The group generated a bounty of ideas, such as the first public library, volunteer fire departments, the first public hospital, police departments, and paved streets. They also collaborated to execute on opportunities. For example, one idea that emerged from the Junto was the need for a liberal arts higher education that would blend study of the classics with practical knowledge. Franklin teamed up with fellow Junto member William Coleman and several others to start what is now the University of Pennsylvania. It was the first multidisciplinary university in America.

Benjamin Franklin is often remembered as driven, self-educated, and endlessly inventive—a quintessential entrepreneur. But what we find most entrepreneurial about Franklin has less to do with his personal talents and traits and more to do with how he facilitated the talents of others. Franklin believed that if he brought together a bunch of smart people in a relaxed atmosphere and let the conversation flow, good opportunities would emerge. He set in motion a trend that the French writer Alexis de Tocqueville noted in *Democracy in America,* his 1835 classic assessment of the young United States: nothing was as distinctive about America as its people's proclivity to form associations around interests, causes, and values.

By the early 1900s, human networks were booming. At his death, J. P. Morgan—one of the most entrepreneurial businessmen of his time—belonged to nearly twenty-four different associations. A Chicago attorney named Paul Harris may not be as famous as Morgan, but his impact is arguably comparable. In search of more clients for his law practice and a cure for his loneliness, he brought together a group of local businesspeople who could help one another in their careers and enjoy one another's fellowship. They called their group Rotary because the location of their weekly meeting rotated among the members. As the club grew in size, to maintain informality, they fined members who addressed other members by anything but their first name. No surnames or titles or "Mister" allowed.[7] Today, there are more than 1.2 million remarkably engaged members in 30,000 Rotary clubs around the world.

In the last quarter of the twentieth century, informal networks were still proliferating, particularly in some of the great innovation hubs in the country. In 1975 a group of microcomputer enthusiasts in the Bay Area formed the Homebrew Computer Club and invited those who shared their interests in technology to "come to a gathering of people with like-minded interests. Exchange information, swap ideas, help work on a project, whatever."[8] Five hundred young geeks joined, and of them, twenty went on to start computer companies, including Steve Wozniak, who cofounded Apple. Homebrew helped establish the distinctly Silicon Valley model of disseminating opportunities and information through informal networks (something we'll discuss in the Network Intelligence chapter).

Small, informal networks are still uniquely efficient at circulating ideas. It's why we still have local PTAs and alumni groups from schools. Book groups. Beekeeping clubs. Conferences and industry meetings. *If you want to increase your opportunity flow, join and participate in as many of these groups and associations as possible.* If you don't know where to start, go to www.meetup.com. Meetup helps ninety thousand interest groups in forty-five thousand cities organize events to bring like-minded people together. Scott Heiferman, Meetup's CEO, says, "DIY is becoming DIO: do it ourselves. More people are turning to each other to make things happen." This is I^{We} in action. Ben and I participate in myriad conferences and meetups. In fact, we first met at an unconventional retreat that brings together one hundred individuals once a year to discuss issues ranging from science to politics to practical philosophy. No speakers, no panels—just brainstorming and networking in the informal setting of Sundance, Utah.

Maximizing your experience at meetups can take some ingenuity. Chris Sacca knows a thing or two about this. Today he is an investor in tech start-ups. But before investing and before working at Google, he was an out-of-work attorney needing income to help him pay off student loans. He started sneaking in through the back door of networking and tech industry events, utilizing his Spanish-language skills to smooth-talk the workers in the kitchen to let him in. Once he realized that handing his new acquaintances a business card that listed only his name wasn't impressing anyone, he hatched a clever plan to boost his credibility at the events he attended: create a consulting firm and employ himself there. He made new business cards, hired a developer to build a website, and enlisted a friend to draw a corporate logo. Then he went to the same networking events with new business cards that read, "Chris Sacca, Principal, Salinger Group." Suddenly, the people he met were interested in talking more. Through these connections he eventually landed an executive job at a Web infrastructure company, and his career took flight.

You don't always have to approach groups as an outsider. There are plenty of networks at your fingertips where you are already an insider—you just have to be a little creative. Think about alumni groups. Sure, high school and college alumni associations are indeed good sources of opportunities. But you're also an alumnus from *organizations* you've worked at in the past.

My membership in a notable corporate alumni group in Silicon Valley has opened the door to a number of breakout opportunities. After eBay acquired PayPal, the members of the PayPal executive team each moved on to new projects but stayed connected, investing in one another's companies, hiring one another, sharing office space, and the like. There are no membership dues, no secret handshakes, no monthly meetings; just informal collaboration. Yet these connections have spawned some of the most successful projects in Silicon Valley. As a result, the group got the name "the PayPal mafia."

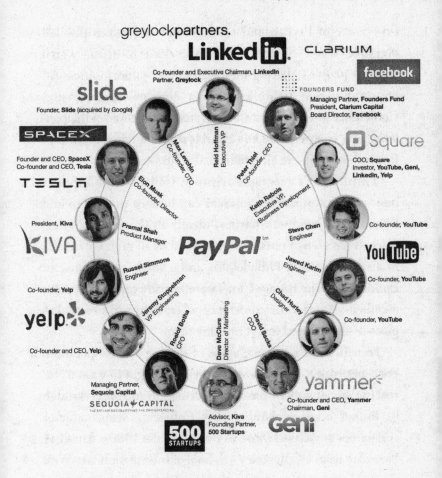

What is it about this network that makes it such a uniquely rich source of opportunities?

First, each individual is high-quality. This is fundamental: A group is only as good as its members. The network is only as good as its nodes. Evaluate a group by evaluating the individual people.

Second, the gang has something in common—the shared

experience of PayPal, and the interests and values that led everyone there. Shared experiences lead to trust, which leads to people's sharing information and opportunities. All opportunity-rich networks have a common denominator. Conference attendees are all interested in the topic of the conference; a congregation at a church shares a faith; Franklin's Junto members were all intellectually curious.

Third, there's geographic density. Collaboration happens best when information and ideas can bounce quickly to and from all the interested parties, ideally in the same physical place. That's why Franklin assembled a small group of friends in a single room in Philadelphia and a single coffeehouse in London. It's why Rotary Clubs were initially capped at twelve members. It's why the conference where Ben and I met takes place in an enclosed resort in a tiny town.

Fourth, there's a strong ethos of sharing and cooperation. For a network to be valuable, everyone has got to want to invest in that network by pushing information and ideas through it. In her book explaining how California semiconductor companies surpassed those in Boston in the 1980s, AnnaLee Saxenian from UC Berkeley's School of Information says West Coast entrepreneurs were inclined to share their discoveries with others, even with competitors, in the spirit of collective progress. In the PayPal group there's a similar dynamic. Folks stay in touch and collaborate, even in cases where there's competition (e.g., there are multiple VCs who sometimes compete for the same deals).

One of the biggest opportunities of my career was the chance to start LinkedIn in 2003. A mere five months after eBay acquired PayPal, I had assembled a team of six people working full-time in an office. I was able to get the business off the ground so quickly because I had a network of friends to serve as cofounders, early employees, and investors. I asked two former colleagues from Socialnet, a former college classmate, and a former colleague from Fujitsu to cofound the company with me. Peter Thiel and Keith Rabois from the PayPal mafia and a few others invested in the business. A former colleague from PayPal even provided LinkedIn's first office space. An appropriate founding for a business with the tagline RELATIONSHIPS MATTER.

To recap some of the qualities of the PayPal mafia: high-quality people, a common bond, an ethos of sharing and cooperation, concentrated in a region and industry. These make it rich in opportunity flow, and the same factors make any network and association worth your while.

Finally, the only thing better than joining groups is starting your own. Start your own mafia—your own group, meetup, or association with PayPal mafia characteristics. Once a year I co-organize something I call the Weekend to Be Named Later, a Franklin-inspired gathering of ambitious friends, to brainstorm ways to change the world. Since 2006 Ben has co-run a Junto modeled after Franklin's original: a couple dozen folks (mainly from the tech industry) meet regularly over lunch to talk shop. The gatherings are focused yet informal, like Franklin's. A laid-back atmosphere encourages candor, intellectual risk taking, and ultimately leads to the generation of better and more interesting ideas. It doesn't even have to be a regular thing. Organizing a Saturday brunch with a dozen ex-coworkers from your previous company only offers upside. And don't forget, when you are the creator and central node of a group, it's like having a courtside seat at a basketball game: you won't miss a thing.

Steven Johnson says, "Chance favors the connected mind." Connect your mind to as many networks as did Benjamin Franklin, Joseph Priestley, J. P. Morgan, and others, and you'll be one step closer to spotting and seizing those game-changing opportunities that great careers are made of.

Do the Hustle

No matter where you are in your career, there will be moments when you feel like your back is against the wall. When you feel like you're going nowhere. When you may be short on funds or allies or both. When no one is knocking at your door inviting you to stuff. These situations call for the most entrepreneurial opportunity-generating strategy of this chapter: hustle. (*Hustler* is bad, but *hustle* is all good.) Many of the people we've met in this book have had to hustle for career opportunities. For example, when Mary Sue Milliken was trying to get the job at Le Perroquet, the fancy Chicago restaurant, she wrote the owner a letter every three or four days for a couple weeks until he hired her (at $3.25 an hour). When her job description said to start at 8:00 a.m., she got to the restaurant at 5:30 a.m. every day.[9] This ethos is what we mean when we talk about hustle, and your ability to do it well can comprise a competitive advantage. Entrepreneurs, forever operating with constraints, are the kings and queens of hustle, and the best examples of hustle in action.

Be Resourceful: If You Don't Have a Bed to Sleep On, Make Your Own

It was January 2008. Airbnb founders Joe Gebbia, Brian Chesky, and Nathan Blecharczyk had a problem: they were broke. They started "Air Bed and Breakfast" thinking that anyone with an air mattress, extra couch, or bed should be able to make money renting out that space on a temporary basis. It wasn't a bad idea. For example, during the 2008 Democratic National Convention in Denver, Colorado, Barack Obama spoke at a packed NFL stadium with eighty thousand seats in a city with a total of twenty-seven thousand quickly-sold-out hotel rooms. Thousands of Democratic supporters were scrambling to find a place to stay. Using Airbnb.com, Denver residents absorbed the excess demand by renting out their couches or beds to visitors. Unfortunately, while the website's usage spiked during the occasional big event or conference, it never gained enough day-to-day traction to make a profitable business. To close the gap between revenue and expenses, the founders maxed out four credit cards and blew through all of their savings.

But they still believed in their idea, and wanted to buy more time to figure out a way to scale the business. So they did what any hustling entrepreneur would do: they sold cereal. Riding presidential election fever, the founders drew upon their Rhode Island School of Design connections and developed custom-designed cereal boxes branded Obama O's ("The Breakfast of Change") and Capn' McCains ("A Maverick in Every Bite"). They folded the boxes in their kitchen, filled 'em with cereal, and sold them online for $40 a pop. Chesky remembers his mom asking him, "So, you're running a cereal company now?" No, they just needed cash—any cash would do. CNN ran a story on the election-season bites, and it wasn't long before they sold out of Obama O's, netting $20,000 in profit.

Extra cash in the bank bought them enough time to figure out how to increase and sustain enough customers to turn a consistent profit. And their resourcefulness impressed enough investors that they were able to raise outside financing, including a Series A investment that I led with Greylock. Hundreds of thousands of travelers have since happily stayed on the bed or air mattress of a host.

It's hard to capture the essence of resourcefulness, but most of us know it when we see it. When Amazon CEO Jeff Bezos was looking for a wife, he told friends who were setting him up on dates that he wanted a woman who was resourceful. But they didn't get it. So he told them, "I want a woman who could help me get out of a Third World prison!" That did the trick.[10] The Airbnb guys, if they had to, could probably break out of a Third World prison.

Be Resilient: When the Naysayers Are Loud, Turn Up the Music

Tim Westergren might be the most resilient man in Silicon Valley. He was inspired to start Internet radio business Pandora back in 1999 after hearing that Geffen Music dropped singer Aimee Mann from their label because she didn't have enough paying fans. Westergren believed if Aimee Mann could be paired in an online directory with very similar yet more popular artists in an online directory, her fan base would broaden. He created the Music Genome Project, in which experts analyze songs, one at a time, on two hundred to four hundred dimensions, and then recommend to users new songs and artists based on the songs and artists they already like. Mann's hit single "Save Me," for example, contains "subtle use of strings" and "mixed major and minor key tonality" and therefore is paired on Pandora with "Fallen" by Sarah McLachlan, which features similar instrumentation.

Skeptics of Pandora were legion. You're going to have individual experts listen to hundreds of thousands of songs and individually assign hundreds of characteristics? You're going to negotiate with the record industry to stream copyrighted music over the Web? You're going to grow an Internet business in the ashes of the dot-com bust? *Puh-lease*. And for nine years, the skeptics were right.

Westergren started Pandora during the first dot-com boom with an infusion of cash from investors. But once the bubble burst, raising additional money to keep the company afloat became impossible given the volatile online music industry and sluggish economy. He started holding a meeting with his fifty or so employees every two weeks, begging them to work unpaid for two more weeks. In late 2002 he arrived at his office to find an eviction notice on the door. In late 2003 four former employees sued him over their deferred salaries. By March 2004, after pitching venture capitalists more than three hundred times, he convinced Walden Venture Capital to lead a

$9 million investment. In 2005, still unprofitable, he changed the business model to rely on money from advertisements as opposed to paid subscriptions. This helped for a time, until March 2007, when the federal Copyright Royalty Board raised the rates online radio stations must pay the labels, a move that threatened to increase Pandora's operating costs by 1,000 percent. "Overnight our business was broken," Westergren says. "We contemplated pulling the plug."[11] But the resilient team partnered with other Internet radio companies and marshaled a massive lobbying effort in Washington to extend the period during which they could negotiate with labels. Westergren's users flooded Congress with emails and phone calls; he estimates about one million emails or phone calls fighting the increase in costs were sent to legislators in total.

In 2009, long after Pandora had been relegated to the "dead pool" of Silicon Valley start-ups, the artists and record labels struck a significant revenue-sharing deal with online broadcasters like Pandora, resolving the royalty dispute. Shortly thereafter, Greylock's David Sze led a new investment in the company and joined the board. By the end of 2010, Pandora offered more than 700,000 songs in its library and had earned $100 million in revenue. The company IPO'd in 2011.

For almost ten years, Pandora was beaten and battered by lawsuits, unfavorable legislation, and the constant threat of bankruptcy. Remarkably, Tim and his team hung in there, in pursuit of the opportunity to change the way people find and listen to music. Resilience and tenacity have kept them in the game, and they can do the same for you in your career.

Both the Airbnb and Pandora teams were all at one point operating with severe resource constraints. They lacked money. They lacked know-how. They lacked connections. They lacked employees, advisors, partners. But could these ostensibly negative constraints have actually enhanced their ability to generate killer opportunities? Potentially. When you have no resources, you create them. When you have no choice but to fight, you fight hard. When you have no choice but to create, you create. Caterina Fake, the cofounder of Flickr, says that the "less money you have, the fewer people and resources you have, the more creative you have to become." Get resourceful or die. Start-ups tend to outmaneuver big companies on breakthrough innovation for this reason: If Microsoft doesn't hustle one year, it will still count billions of dollars in the bank; if the start-up doesn't hustle, it's game over. If you want to find out how resourceful you can be, shrink your budget. Move your deadlines up. See how you cope. This may make you more resilient to actual hardships that inevitably arise.

●　●　●

Selling cereal to fund an online directory of available couches and air mattresses? Flooding Congress with one million emails and phone calls to reverse a law that would bankrupt your company? Call it resourcefulness, resilience, chutzpah, or hustle—whatever it's called, it's the entrepreneurial way to create opportunities for yourself in tough times. Hustle is not something you can study in a textbook. But it is something you can be inspired to do more of. And like most of the other entrepreneurial strategies in this book, the more you hustle, the more second nature it becomes.

Eric Barker is a man who exemplifies entrepreneurial hustle in his career, and he's never started a company and never lived in Silicon Valley. After a decade working as a screenwriter in Hollywood, Eric decided to go back to school and get an MBA. He'd enjoyed a good deal of success in Hollywood—including work at top studios like Disney—but wanted to build management skills. So in the fall of 2007, Eric enrolled in Boston College's business school, where he took on a full class load, and a summer internship at Nintendo. The following fall, he began to search for a job at a management level.

Then the economy collapsed. Sure, he had an impressive résumé and held fancy degrees from good schools, but none of it seemed to matter to prospective employers. They all said they wanted someone with a stronger finance background. Five months later, with still no job opportunities in sight, he posted an ad to Facebook targeted to other users employed at five companies: Microsoft, Apple, Netflix, YouTube, and IDEO (a design and innovation consultancy based in Palo Alto). The ad featured his picture and title and read as follows: "Hi, my name is Eric and my dream is to work for Microsoft. I'm a MBA/MFA with a strong media background. Can you help me? Please click!"

He didn't truly believe anyone would, so you can imagine his surprise when, within weeks, his inbox was filled with emails from strangers sending him encouragement and, more important, the names of people they knew at Microsoft. Soon, Eric's story hit the blogosphere. In an awesome twist, Eric hustled to get attention . . . about his hustling. He sent more than one hundred emails out to various media outlets and bloggers telling his posting-an-ad-on-social-network-to-find-a-job story. Before long, it was picked up everywhere from the *Boston Globe* to the *Baltimore Sun*.

His ad was viewed more than fifty thousand times, garnered five hundred clicks, and generated twenty emails from recruiters offering to submit his résumé to contacts looking to connect on LinkedIn to learn more about him. He was getting a lot of attention, to be sure, but still no job. Then in June 2009, roughly six weeks after placing the ad, the tide turned: Eric received that long-awaited email from a recruiter at Microsoft. While he didn't end up going to Microsoft—he ultimately landed a job at a video design company via an introduction from one of his business school professors—the whole experience taught him something important. Taking an analogy from his past life, he shared with us about the key insight that launched the chain of events: "The HR department is like the soldiers in the movie *300,* holding the line. They have no power to say 'yes' but enormous power to say 'no.' Their job is to prevent you from moving forward. Find a way to vault past them by getting introductions to people who can say 'yes.' It's what I did—I hustled."

• • •

Breakout opportunities come and go—if you don't seize them, you lose them. After the eBay/PayPal deal in 2003, I had a plan to take a year off and do some travel. To clear my head and plot the year ahead, I first took a two-week vacation to Australia. While there I reflected on the moment—and I concluded I needed to return to Silicon Valley and start a consumer Internet company as soon as possible. There was a window of opportunity I could not afford to miss. For one, the market conditions were ripe. There was lots of innovation still to be done on the consumer Web, yet many entrepreneurs (possible competitors) and investors were on the sidelines, scarred from the dot-com burst. They wouldn't be on the sidelines forever. Also, my network was strong coming off the PayPal win, and I could relatively quickly organize the resources to get a new company launched.

The lesson is that great opportunities almost never fit your schedule. It would be nice if you came upon that killer job opportunity right when you were thinking about leaving your current job. It would be nice if that exclusive conference coincided with the week your boss happens to be away. Usually, the timing is imperfect and difficult. Most often, you'll be in the middle of a different plan—like about to set off on an around-the-world trip.

And in addition to being inconvenient, the opportunity you generate or find will likely be shrouded in ambiguity and uncertainty. Frequently, it won't be completely clear that it's better than another opportunity. You may be tempted to "keep your options open" and continue to mull things over, as opposed to committing to the breakout you think you've identified or generated. That would be a mistake. "Keeping your options open" is frequently more of a risk than committing to a plan of action.

Many failures in results can be chalked up to people trying to keep their options open. As my dad once told me, *making a decision reduces opportunities in the short run, but increases opportunities in the long run*. To move forward in your career, you have to *commit* to specific opportunities as part of an iterative plan, despite doubt and despite inconvenience.

If not now, when?

INVEST IN YOURSELF

In the next day:

- Budget time for randomness. Deliberately underschedule yourself for a day next week to read a book you wouldn't otherwise read, take a coworker in a different department out for lunch, or attend a speech or seminar in a different but related field.

- Ask the most curious person you know out to lunch, and try to get infected by their sense of awe.

In the next week:

- Find an industry event or ideas conference to attend in the next six months. Book your ticket and transportation to the event.

- Set aside one full day coming up to be a "yes day." Say "yes" all day and note the serendipity that comes of it.

- Opportunities are attached to people. Identify the people in your network who always seem to have their hands in interesting pots. Try to understand what makes them hubs of opportunity and resolve to meet more people with those characteristics.

In the next month:

- Start your own group or association. Maybe a regular luncheon or simply a one-time meetup—what's important is that you try to convene friends to share ideas and resources. Set up a simple wiki or use LinkedIn groups or events to organize and share the details.

• Subscribe to magazines like *Wired* or the *MIT Technology Review* and others like them—they tend to show a glimpse at what's next. Identify friends who are early technology adopters. The goal? Understand how technological, economic, or social trends might create waves of new opportunities.

Network Intelligence

Have an explicit conversation with your allies about how to collaborate on finding, generating, and exploiting great opportunities. Tell your allies that if you come upon a good opportunity, you'll try hard to involve them in it.

6
Take Intelligent Risks

Risk tends to get a bad rap. We associate it with things like losing money in the stock market, or riding a motorcycle without a helmet. But risk isn't the enemy—it's a permanent part of life. In fact, being proactively intelligent about risk is a prerequisite for seizing those breakout opportunities we talked about in the last chapter. Many more people would enjoy breakout opportunities if it were only a matter of tapping networks, courting serendipity, and being resourceful. The reality is that doing those things is usually necessary but rarely enough. There's *competition* for good opportunities. And because of that, if you can intelligently take on risk, you will find opportunities others miss. Where others see a red light, you'll see green.

"Risk" in a career context is the downside consequences from a given action or decision, and the likelihood that the downside actually occurs. Risky situations, then, are those in which the risk level crosses a threshold. For example, flying on a commercial airplane of a major airline is not risky because while the downside scenario of a crash is painful, the likelihood of a crash is extremely low. Meanwhile, the reward of rapid transit is significant. There's *risk* when you get on a plane, but it's so low that commercial flights are not *risky*.

Some entrepreneurs are irrational risk takers: cowboy types willing to bet the farm in pursuit of some crazy dream. But what sets the great entrepreneurs apart from the pack is not a high tolerance for risk per se, but their ability to judiciously assess and manage it. They strategically pursue only those opportunities with enough upside to justify the possible downside. It's one of the key skills that makes entrepreneurs successful.

Risk is the flip side of every opportunity and career move. When George Clooney aggressively auditioned and sold himself for *ER*, it was a risk: the show could have been a high-profile flop. Confronting your boss about a problem you're having with a coworker involves the risk of getting on his bad side. Negotiating for a higher salary involves the risk of seeming greedy. Freelancing on the side comes with the risk that your performance at your day job will suffer. "[I]f you are not genuinely pained by the risk involved in your strategic choices, it's not much of a strategy," says Reed Hastings of Netflix. This is as true for careers as it is for business. If you don't have to seriously think about the risk involved in a career opportunity, it's probably not the breakout opportunity you're looking for.

The constant presence of risk is why every career Plan A should be accompanied by a Plan B and Plan Z. Of course, risk isn't confined to career-related activities. Doing *anything* contains risk, including things we do every day, like going for a jog in the park or living in a world where there are nuclear weapons and earthquakes. Even inaction contains risk. A sick person who chooses not to see a doctor is taking on a risk by doing nothing. Inaction is especially risky in a changing world that demands adaptation (see the American auto industry, for example).

So we are *all* risk takers. But we are not all equally intelligent about how we do it. Many people think you get career stability by minimizing all risk. But ironically, in a changing world, that's one of the riskiest things you can do. Others think acknowledging downside possibilities is a sign of weakness: "Failure is not an option!" may make for a good movie line, but it's not good when formulating strategy. Rather than avoiding risk, if you take *intelligent* risks, it will give you a competitive edge.

ASSESSING AND MANAGING RISK

Learning how to accurately assess the level of risk in a situation isn't easy, for a few reasons. First, risk is both personal and situational. What may be risky to you may not be risky to someone else. There are people for whom quitting a job before having another one lined up is unacceptably risky; for others, it's a fine proposition. There are people who forego earning income for several months to start their own companies; others wouldn't dream of putting themselves in a situation where they aren't guaranteed a steady salary and benefits.

What's more, risk is dynamic. You are changing, the competition is changing, the world is changing. What may be risky to you right now may not be a month or year or five years from now. What's the risk of ruffling your colleagues' feathers if you lobby aggressively for a lead role on a project? It depends on murky factors that are always in flux. If you just got a raise and upgrade to your title, for example, it's a different calculus than if you're new on the job. Nothing is universally risky or not risky; it's a matter of degree and it various tremendously based on situation and personality.[1]

Assessing risk, while always difficult, is not impossible. Entrepreneurs do it every day. But they don't use fancy risk-analysis models like those found on Wall Street. And neither should you. There's no mathematical formula that could possibly capture the probabilities and range of outcomes of a dynamic start-up, let alone the dynamic start-up that is your career. It's impossible to quantify the pros and cons of every opportunity. You will have time constraints. You will have information constraints. Moreover, your intuition is riddled with cognitive biases that get in the way of rational assessment. So here are a few principles to keep in mind to help you evaluate how risky an opportunity really is, and how you manage the risk that does exist.

Overall, it's probably not as risky as you think.

Most people overrate risk. At our core we humans are wired to avoid risk. We evolved this way because to our ancestors, it was more costly to miss the sign of a predator (threat) than to miss the sign of food (opportunity). Neuropsychologist Rick Hanson puts it this way: "To keep our ancestors alive, Mother Nature evolved a brain that routinely tricked them into making three mistakes: overestimating threats, underestimating opportunities, and underestimating resources (for dealing with threats and fulfilling opportunities)." The result is that we're programmed to overestimate the risk in any given situation.[2]

Sticks get our attention a lot faster than carrots do. Psychologists call this *negativity bias,* and it pops up all the time in day-to-day life. One stern warning to avoid working with a person makes a stronger impression than one glowing recommendation. Anxiety about how your boss will react to an unconventional proposal will overpower feelings of optimism that he'll be impressed by your work.

Overestimating threats and avoiding losses may be a fine strategy for achieving evolution's cold mandate to pass our genes on to future generations. But it's not the way to make the most of this life. To lead a big and vigorous life, you must work to overcome this negativity bias. The first step is to remind yourself that the downside of a given situation is probably not as bad, or as likely, as it seems.

Is the worst-case scenario tolerable or intolerable?

Of the voluminous research on risk, remarkably little of it actually analyzes how real businesspeople make real decisions in the real world. An exception is a study done by professor Zur Shapira in 1991. He asked about seven hundred high-level executives from the United States and Israel to describe how they think about risk in different scenarios. What he found likely came as a disappointment to architects of fancy decision trees. The executives surveyed didn't calculate the mathematical expected value of various scenarios. They didn't draft long lists of pros and cons. Instead, most simply tried to get a handle on a single yes-or-no question: Could they tolerate the outcome if the worst-case scenario happened? So the first thing you want to ask of a possible opportunity is, If the worst-case scenario happens, would I still be in the game? If the worst-case scenario is the serious tarnishing of your reputation, or loss of all your economic assets, or something otherwise career-ending, don't accept that risk. If the worst-case scenario is getting fired, losing a little bit of time or money, or experiencing discomfort, as long as you have a solid and reliable Plan Z in place, you will still be in the game, and should be open to taking on that risk.

Can you change or reverse the decision midway through? Is Plan B doable?

Management consulting firms frequently offer to pay for analysts to go to business school in exchange for a two-year commitment to work at the firm after graduation. Analysts who take the offer are making a four-year commitment in total: two years in school, two years at the same firm afterward. Precommitting four years of your life is riskier than career choices that allow you to pivot to Plan B if you decide something is not going well or if some other amazing opportunity came up. So when assessing a risk, if you realize you made a mistake, could you reverse your decision easily? Could you get to a Plan B or Plan Z relatively quickly? If the answer is no, the opportunity is riskier and should be approached more cautiously.

Michael Dell famously dropped out of the University of Texas to start Dell Computer. But his start-up wasn't a sure thing at the time, so he managed the risk by hedging his bets. Instead of dropping out of college for good, he applied for a formal leave of absence so that if the company seemed to be going south, he could return to his studies with no problem.[3] Dell took a prudent risk that preserved the option to reverse his decision and go to Plan B.

You'll never be fully certain. Don't conflate uncertainty with risk.

There will always be uncertainty about career opportunities and risks. Uncertainty is an ingredient of risk. And the more compelling and complex the opportunity, the more uncertainty tends to surround it. In all situations, you simply cannot know everything about all possible pros and cons. While you don't want to make career moves on 0 percent information, you also don't want to wait till you have 100 percent information—or else you'll wait forever. Uncertainty makes people uncomfortable. But uncertainty does not automatically mean something is risky. Jetting off to vacation in Hawaii with no set itinerary introduces many uncertainties about what will transpire, but it's not particularly risky. After all, how likely are you to have a bad time in Hawaii? When Sheryl Sandberg came to Silicon Valley from Washington, there were innumerable uncertainties. (Would California be a good place to raise a family? How would her reputation suffer if Google was a flop?) Had she treated all the unknowables associated with entering a new industry as serious risks, she would never have joined Google and would have missed out on a breakout opportunity.

When it's not clear how something will play out, many people avoid it altogether. But the biggest and best opportunities frequently are the ones with the most question marks. Don't let uncertainty lull you into overestimating the risk.

Consider age and stage. What will the risks be to you in a few years?

Age and career stage affect your level of risk. Generally, the downside consequence of failure is lower the younger you are. If you make mistakes in your twenties and thirties, you have plenty of time to recover both financially and reputationally. You have parents and family to fall back on. You are less likely to have kids or a mortgage. Just as financial advisors counsel young people to invest in stocks more than bonds, it's important to be especially aggressive accepting career risk when you are young. This is a main reason many young people start companies, travel around the world, and do other relatively "high-risk" career moves: the downside is lower. If something worthwhile will be riskier in five years than it is now, be more aggressive about taking it on now. As you age and build more assets, your risk tolerance shifts.

Pursue Opportunities Where Others Misperceive the Risk

There will be times when what's risky to someone else is not risky to you because your particular characteristics and circumstances make it a different analysis. Risk is personal. But there will also be times when people like you—people with similar assets, aspirations, and operating within the same market realities—will perceive something as riskier than it actually is. This creates an opening for you to go after an opportunity that your peers may be unwisely avoiding.

Warren Buffett has a mantra: "Be fearful when others are greedy and greedy when others are fearful." It's a competitive edge for him. During the 2008 financial crisis, Buffett bought U.S. stocks cheap when most Americans were scared and selling. You make money in the stock market when you believe something others do not. You buy a stock because you believe its price will be *higher* in the future than it is today. The sellers of such a stock believe the stock's price will be *lower* in the future than it is today. In public market investing, as in many things, you achieve big success when *you're both contrarian and right*.

To be contrarian and right about risk taking means you don't just jump at the obvious high-risk, high-reward opportunities. Rather, you pursue opportunities that have a lower risk than your peers think, but which are still high-reward.

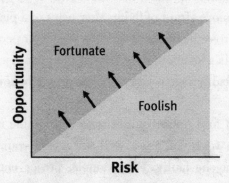

Common career opportunities or situations like this include:

- *Jobs that pay less in cash but offer tremendous learning.* People focus on easily quantifiable hard assets—like how much they're getting paid in cash. Jobs that offer less cash but more learning are too quickly dismissed as risky.

- *Part-time or contract gigs that are less "stable" than full-time jobs.* A little bit of volatility is less problematic than people think; in fact, it's good, as we discuss in the next section. Many dismiss part-time jobs and contract gigs as being inferior to full-time work, but in reality, they are a terrific way to build the skills and relationships that help you pivot into a wide range of Plan B's.

- *Hiring someone without much experience but who's a fast learner and much cheaper.* This is a medium risk with high potential reward: fast learners can make up their inexperience. They tend to be undervalued by the market.

- *An opportunity where the risks are highly publicized.* Thanks to our innate negativity bias, the more we *hear* about the downside to something, the more likely we are to overestimate the probability that it will occur (this is why people tend to become more afraid of flying after news of a plane crash is splashed across the headlines). If the media, or people in your industry, talk a lot about the riskiness of a certain job or career path, it probably isn't as risky as most people believe.

You can find opportunities with a favorable risk/reward dynamic in areas you know well and where your peers' risk calculus may be faulty. For example, novice entrepreneurs sometimes freak out during a recession, bailing on their start-up idea because they think raising money is harder, getting customers to spend money is harder, and that a corporate job is more secure in difficult times. Experienced entrepreneurs know that in reality starting a company in a down economy has a lower risk than people think, precisely because other people are scared off by the risk. When you start a company in a recession there's less competition for top-notch talent, customer dollars, press coverage, and more. Many incredible companies, such as Microsoft and FedEx, were started in the depths of a recession. That so many entrepreneurs perceive recession timing as high-risk actually makes it lower-risk.

What are the settings where you have a privileged position and better-than-average information to assess risk?

SHORT-TERM RISK INCREASES LONG-TERM STABILITY

It's generally assumed that certain careers are riskier than others. In 2003, in a paper called "Risk and Career Choice," two economists estimated the riskiness of working in different industries according to the consistency of income streams and average unemployment levels of people in those careers.[4] They referred to income fluctuations, including bouts of unemployment, as "shocks." By their account, risky careers (more severe shocks) included business, entertainment, and sales. Non-risky careers (less severe shocks) included education, health care, and engineering. Another way of expressing this is that risky careers were thought to be more volatile and nonrisky careers were thought to be more stable. These results jibe with conventional wisdom—risk-averse people may be teachers or doctors (or lawyers or bankers), whereas risk-taking people may be starting companies or trying out on Broadway. But is this assumption right?

The Volatility Paradox: Small Fires Prevent the Big Burn

In his book *The Black Swan*, Nassim Taleb writes about the unexpected, rare, high-impact event. The September 11 terrorist attack, the stock market crash in 1987, and the Indian Ocean tsunami in 2004 were black swans. They were impossible to predict beforehand, had a low chance of happening in the first place, and exacted a large impact. Joshua Cooper Ramo, a friend, in his excellent book *The Age of the Unthinkable*, argues that we should expect to see more black swans in our lifetime. Ramo believes the number of unthinkable disruptions in the world is on the rise in part because we've become so globally interconnected that a minor disturbance anywhere can cause disruption everywhere. When Asian or European economies falter, so does the U.S. economy. When there's political upheaval in the Middle East, gas prices soar. Fragility is the price we pay for a hyperlinked world where all the slack is optimized out of the system.

The economy, politics, and job market of the future will host many unexpected shocks. In this sense, the world of tomorrow will be more like the Silicon Valley of today: constant change and chaos. So does that mean you should try to avoid those shocks by going into low-volatility careers

like health care or teaching? Not necessarily. The way to intelligently manage risk is to make yourself resilient to these
shocks by pursuing those opportunities with some volatility
baked in. Taleb argues—furthering an argument popular-
ized by ecologists who study resilience—that the less volatile
the environment, the more destructive a black swan will be
when it comes. Nonvolatile environments give only an illusion
of stability: "Dictatorships that do not appear volatile, like,
say, Syria or Saudi Arabia, face a larger risk of chaos than,
say, Italy, as the latter has been in a state of continual political turmoil since the [Second World War]."[5] Ramo explains
why: Italy is resilient to dangerous chaos because it has absorbed frequent attacks like "small, controlled burns in a forest, clearing away just enough underbrush to make [them]
invulnerable to a larger fire."[6] These small burns strengthen
the political system's capacity to respond to unexpected cri-
ses. Syria or North Korea or Burma do not have small burns;
a fire there could quickly become a devastating catastrophe.
In the short run, low volatility means stability. In the long
run, though, low volatility leads to increased vulnerability,
because it renders the system less resilient to unthinkable external shocks. It's for these reasons that Chicago economist
Raghuram Rajan told a Federal Reserve symposium in 2005
that "perhaps Chairman Greenspan should be faulted for allowing only two mild recessions during his tenure."[7] Without
enough stress tests on the economic system, it became dangerously unresilient to a big fire.

This paradox—high short-term risk leading to low long-
term risk—holds true for careers as well. In the past, when
you thought about stable employers, you thought IBM, HP,

General Motors—all stalwart companies that have been around a long time and employ hundreds of thousands of people. At one point in their history they all had de facto (or even rather explicit) policies of lifetime employment. Imagine what happened, then, when market realities forced the companies to drop pink slips onto the desks of thousands of employees. Imagine what it must have been like for someone who thought he was a lifer at HP; his skills, experience, and network were all inextricably linked to his nine-to-five employer. And then: BOOM. He's unemployed.

While today's employers do not offer lifetime employment—the employer-employee pact has fully disintegrated, as we mentioned at the outset—some industries still offer some semblance of stability: it's relatively hard to be fired, your salary won't fluctuate much, your job responsibilities stay steady. These are the careers generally deemed less risky: government, education, engineering, health care. But compare someone working full-time in state government to an independent real estate agent. The real estate agent doesn't know when his next paycheck is coming in. He has ups and downs. He has to hustle to build a network of clients and keep up with changes in the market. His income is lumpy, and sporadic big wins (selling a multimillion-dollar home) keep him alive. The government worker, by contrast, gets a steady paycheck and an automatic promotion every couple years. He always eats well . . . until the day comes that government pensions explode or austerity measures wipe out his department. Now he's screwed. He will starve because, unlike the real estate agent, he has no idea how to deal with the downs.

Or compare a staff editor at a prestigious magazine to a freelance writer. The staff editor at a magazine enjoys a dependable income stream, regular work, and built-in network. The freelance writer has to hustle every day for gigs, and some months are better than others. The staff editor is always well fed; the freelance writer is hungry on some days. Then the day comes when print finally dies, the magazine industry collapses, and the staff editor gets laid off. Having built up no resilience, he will starve. He's less equipped to bounce to the next thing, whereas the freelance writer has been bouncing around her whole life—she'll be fine. So which type of career is riskier in the long run, in the age of the unthinkable?

Without frequent, contained risk taking, you are setting yourself up for a major dislocation at some point in the future. Inoculating yourself to big risks is like inoculating yourself against the flu virus. By injecting a small bit of flu into your body in the form of a vaccination, you make a big flu outbreak survivable. By introducing regular volatility into your career, you make surprise survivable. You gain the "ability to absorb shocks gracefully."[8]

Some job paths automatically provide regular volatility (e.g., entrepreneurship or freelancing). In other jobs you'll have to introduce shocks and disruptions manually. Do so by aggressively implementing the opportunity-creating strategies we discussed in the previous chapter (opportunity and risk are two sides of the same coin, after all): join and create groups, be in motion, take on side projects, hustle. In a phrase, say "yes" more. What would happen if you defaulted to "yes" for a full day? A full week? If you say yes to the conference invite you were tempted to skip, might you overhear a comment that ignites your imagination for a new business or new research or a new relationship? Perhaps. Might it also lead to some dead ends, mishaps, wastes of time? Sure. But both, in fact, are good: you benefit either from a serendipitous opportunity, or from the resilience you build if nothing immediately comes of it.

Pretending you can avoid risk causes you to miss opportunities that can change your life. It also lulls you into a dangerously fragile life pattern, leaving you exposed to a huge blow-up in the future. What's more, you can never perfectly anticipate when inflection points or any other career-threatening event will occur. When you're resilient, you can play for big opportunities with less worry about the possible consequences of unanticipated hiccups. For the start-up of you, *the only long-term answer to risk is resilience.*

Remember: If you don't find risk, risk will find you.

INVEST IN YOURSELF

In the next day:

- Reflect for a few minutes on risk in your life. Rank the projects you're involved in by risk—from most to least risky. Then think hard about the real downside and upside possibilities and be sure you're not exaggerating the overall riskiness. Where there's uncertainty, are you mistakenly ascribing risk?

In the next week:

- Identify—and take on—risks that are acceptable to you but that others tend to avoid. Are you okay having less money in savings and taking a low-paying but high-learning job? Or maybe a month-to-month employment contract as opposed to something longer term? Go find a project with these sorts of risks. It will differentiate you from others.

In the next month:

- Make a plan to increase the short-term volatility in your life. How can you take on projects—or a new job—that involve more ups and downs, more uncertainty?

- Revisit your Plan Z. Is it still viable? If your Plan A were to unravel, will you still be in the game? Consult mentors in your network to help think through contingencies.

Network Intelligence

Have frank conversations with your allies and other trusted connections about the kind of risks they are able to take on. Knowing their risk calculus will enable you to help them more readily. Also, remember that if your risk assessment on an opportunity is contrarian, other people will be deterred by it. Test how contrarian your idea really is by gauging how your network reacts to it!

7

Who You Know Is What You Know

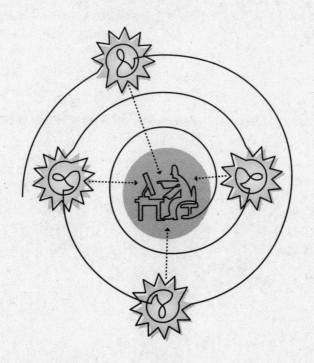

A decade ago, Bill Gates wrote: "The most meaningful way to differentiate your company from your competition, the best way to put distance between you and the crowd, is to do an outstanding job with information. *How you gather, manage, and use information will determine whether you win or lose.*"[1] This could not be truer today. But the way we've been socialized to think about information and knowledge is radically insufficient. Our educational system trains us to memorize facts stored in textbooks and then regurgitate them on an exam. This formal philosophy of learning treats knowledge like a fixed asset: learn, then you have it forever! But as a modern professional, you can't acquire knowledge this way, because the knowledge you need isn't static—it's always changing. You can't cram your brain with all the relevant information that might possibly be relevant to your careers, then deploy it on exam day. In the world of work, every day is exam day—every day brings new, unpredictable challenges and decisions. Stockpiling facts won't get you anywhere. *What will get you somewhere is being able to access the information you need, when you need it.*

NAVIGATE PROFESSIONAL CHALLENGES WITH NETWORK INTELLIGENCE

Entrepreneurs navigate the day-to-day issues of running a company by gathering *intelligence*: actionable, timely information on all facets of their business, including industry trends, opportunities, competitors' activities, customer sentiment, promising young talent, and sales trends. In a business, intelligence serves as a GPS device.

You need good intelligence to run the start-up of you. The preceding chapters should have prompted questions in your mind like: How desirable are my skills in the changing market? How do I know when I should pivot into a new industry niche? What are the best job opportunities and how do I exploit them? These are not easy questions. They're certainly not questions you can answer by merely reflecting for a few minutes or filling out a worksheet. You, too, need business intelligence to navigate these challenges.

You get it by talking to people in your network. It's *people* who help you understand your assets, aspirations, and the market realities; it's *people* who help you vet and get introduced to possible allies and trust connections; it's *people* who help you track the risk attached to a given opportunity. I^{We} is the formula for gathering the kind of information that will help you navigate professional challenges.

What you get when you tap in to other people's brains is called *network intelligence*. There's plenty of good information to be found in books and magazines and search engines.

Yet your network is frequently a better—and sometimes the only—fount of pivotal intelligence. A book can't tell you what skills you need to excel in a certain market niche. A magazine can't help you weigh the risks of moving halfway around the world for a job. A search engine can't introduce you to the networks that dish breakout opportunities. But, your network can.

You have had a network full of intelligence for as long as you've had friends. But until very recently, tapping this intelligence required time-intensive tasks like maintaining an up-to-date Rolodex, sending written letters, and arranging in-person meetings. Networks and networking were always associated with job hunting because it was so costly in time and effort to deploy your network that you'd only do it for really important things—like finding a job. But now it's easy and inexpensive to access the information bouncing around the brains of our connections. With everyone connected, the transaction costs of engaging your network are so low that it makes sense to pull intelligence from your network not only for the big career challenges—like finding a good job—but on a broad range of day-to-day issues.

The individuals we've met in previous chapters turned to their network on a regular basis as they navigated their careers. When Sheryl Sandberg was working for Larry Summers at the World Bank, Summers recalls asking Sheryl to research what the effects might have been of a bailout in 1917 in Russia. "What most students would have done," Summers told Ken Auletta in *The New Yorker*, "is gone off to the library, skimmed some books on Russian history, and said they weren't sure it was possible. What Sheryl did was call Richard Pipes," a Harvard historian who specialized in the Russian Revolution. "She engaged him for one hour and took detailed notes." Which she impressed Summers with the following day.[2]

Your network is an indispensable source of intelligence because people offer private observations and impressions that would never appear in a public place like the *Wall Street Journal* or even your company newsletter. Only a coworker can clue you in to your boss's idiosyncratic preferences. Only a friend working in another organization can tell you about an as-yet-unannounced job position being created there.

Second, people offer personalized, contextualized advice. Friends and acquaintances know your interests and can tailor their information and advice accordingly. For example, if you're trying to weigh the pros and cons of taking a job that entails a significant drop in salary, people who know you well will be able to judge whether or not you can live a leaner lifestyle. After Sheryl Sandberg left the World Bank, she didn't do a Google search to figure out what her next move should be. Instead, she called up the CEO of Google—Eric Schmidt—and picked his brain.

Third, people can filter information you get from other sources. People can tell you *which* books to read; *which* parts of the article are important; *which* search results to ignore; *which* people to trust or not trust. People help focus your attention on the intelligence that's actionable and relevant. In an age of information overload, this is an incredibly valuable benefit.

Finally, many people simply think better thoughts when in dialogue with others. Remember I^{We}: an individual's power is raised exponentially with the help of a network. This is partly because when information moves back and forth between knowledgeable people who care, the signal strengthens. Two (or more) well-coordinated brains beat one every time.

Achieving Network Literacy

For centuries, literacy meant the ability to read and write. Those who could read books—and write them—held the power in a society. Then the Internet came along and massively multiplied the amount of information created and indexed on a daily basis. Power shifted to those who, in addition to being reading-writing literate, could also wade through billions of bits and find the best information online. Author John Battelle calls this *search literacy*—the ability to enter the optimal search terms, wade through the ocean of results, and follow the links that lead to the best information.

Today even search literacy is not enough. The bigger advantage is gained by *network literacy*: knowing how to conceptualize, access, and benefit from the information flowing through your social network. Let's go over the techniques you need to know in order to tap in to it most efficiently and become network literate.

How to Pull Intelligence from Your Network

During the 2011 earthquake and tsunami in Japan, the National Oceanographic and Atmospheric Administration's (NOAA) Tsunami Early Warning Center in Honolulu, Hawaii, shifted into overdrive. The system is a network of sensors located in thirty-nine deep-ocean stations throughout the Pacific and Atlantic Oceans and the Gulf of Mexico. When a sensor determines that the water level at its location exceeds predicted levels for longer than fifteen seconds, the system starts transmitting information to satellites at very short intervals. This information is then relayed to trained scientists on land who use it to determine whether a tsunami has indeed occurred, and if so, its magnitude and the direction it is headed—allowing scientists to send warnings to areas and regions that may be affected.

During that grim day in March, data streamed from sensors located within the NOAA's Pacific Ocean stations. These data were relayed to computers at the Pacific Tsunami Warning Center in Honolulu, Hawaii, where scientists analyzed the information and then issued a series of tsunami watches and warnings.[3] As predicted, a few hours after the earthquake, the waves hit the Waikiki shoreline in Honolulu, a place normally teeming with sunbathers. But thanks to the evacuation orders issued as a result of NOAA's early warning, by the time the waves crashed ashore, everyone in the area had been evacuated.[4]

NOAA's Tsunami Warning System works because it pulls readings from dozens of stations. If there were just a few sensors floating out in the middle of the Pacific Ocean, scientists wouldn't be able to calibrate the direction of the tsunami or know if the wave was gathering strength and speed. However, with data coming in from *multiple* sensors in *multiple* bodies of water, scientists can compare and combine information to draw a variety of conclusions, including when the wave would be expected to hit a coastline.

The information in your network of people is distributed and collected in a similar way. Your coworkers, business colleagues, allies, and acquaintances are each like a unique sensor that can relay different bits of information. They work at different companies, maintain different interests, live in different cities. In the same way that one sensor alone can't tell you very much about the trajectory of a tsunami, one person's feedback or advice or tip isn't enough to inform a decision about your career trajectory. But combine and compare multiple streams of information as the analysts who monitor tsunamis in Hawaii do, and their blended perspectives produce rich intelligence.

In December 2009, the publishing house for which Iris Wong* worked underwent one of the biggest reorganizations in company history. Its six divisions were compressed into four. While only a few dozen people were let go company-wide, and she wasn't among them, she feared whether the reorg was a sign that the worst was yet to come. She wondered whether there would be a job for junior editors in the near future. Should she get out now? Or should she put her head down, work hard, and try to weather the storm? She didn't know. So she talked informally to her coworkers. But being just as rattled by the recent news as she was, they spouted bleak doomsday scenarios, and she wasn't sure whether to take them seriously.

So she called a friend high up at a record label, a business

---

*Iris's name has been changed.

she knew was facing challenges similar to those of the publishing industry. The friend warned that big restructurings of the sort Iris had just experienced were often a sign of further consolidations and layoffs to follow. After all, unless there's a change to a company's business model, short-term cost-cutting measures like layoffs won't fix underlying problems.

Then she called her father, who had worked for decades on Wall Street. He'd witnessed rounds of mergers and acquisitions and layoffs and knew the signs. He told her to look out for a few things: higher-ups more frequently shut behind closed doors, big meetings being put off or moved, visitors from the headquarters of the parent company. Pretty soon these things started happening at the publisher. Moreover, as her father, he knew Iris was a generally anxious person and would be miserable working in an environment where she feared any day could be her last.

So Iris—effectively thinking about her Plan B—emailed all the writers, editors, and publishing refugees she knew and asked if they had any suggestions for related career paths. One response from a former colleague intrigued her: Why not parlay her publishing skills into doing press outreach and social media marketing for a literary public relations company? It happened that her former colleague knew someone she could call, and a few weeks later a boutique firm created a new position for her. Meanwhile, a couple months later, the publisher she used to work for experienced another painful round of layoffs, and many at her level were let go.

If Iris hadn't tapped her network for advice and the connection, she would likely have stayed at her old job out of inertia—and gotten hit by a career tsunami. Instead, she turned a potential inflection point into an opportunity to pivot to another corner of her industry.

Network intelligence isn't useful only in times of trouble. We need it in good times *and* bad, which is why we should be constantly tapping our networks for multiple streams of information about everything from job opportunities to market trends to changes in office dynamics. So how to figure who has the intelligence you need at any given moment, and how to go about extracting it most effectively?

Pose Questions to Your Entire Network

As we saw from Iris's story, there are two basic ways to tap information from your network: (1) ask targeted questions to specific individuals in your network (as when Iris called her friend in the record business, and later her father), and/or (2) cast the net more widely by querying a broad swath of your network all at once (as she did when she sent a mass email to her writer and publishing friends). Technology makes the latter easy. For example, a woman in our extended network recently wanted to know whether it was appropriate to bring up salary on a first job interview. So she posted a poll to her LinkedIn network (see page 204). A broad, relatively generic question such as the one on the next page is best asked as a mass email or as a poll on a social network because many people have relevant experience—lots of people have negotiated salaries and could share helpful anecdotes. Thus you get

Is it appropriate to bring up salary on a first interview?

Sara K. Pennington - 1043 votes - 8 days left

- ○ Yes-definitely
- ○ Maybe-depends on the opportunity
- ○ No-it's not appropriate

Vote   or View Results

Comments   Follow comments ☆

Don

I think a person should go with the flow. You need to provide some hints on what your expectations are with the role and steer the conversation towards the answers you are looking for. Some people can do it well and others need to ask in a direct way.

about 18 hours ago | Flag comment   Voted for Maybe-
depends on the opportunity

Kevin

I agree with Ming-Wei Hung. The onus of research should be on the job hunter. That is what networks are for (LinkedIn for example). Salary is based on the industry, position and location. A Bank Manager in Boise is going to pay less than a Bank Manager in NYC, but it may be a better job. Do your homework, don't waste your time interviewing for a company that will not pay to your expectations. Know what it takes to ask for the expected salary. Your interview is your opportunity to promote your value to the company, including your knowledge of the industry, the company and their competition.

about 19 hours ago | Flag comment   Voted for No-
it's not appropriate

exposed to a large pool and wide range of viewpoints. Plus, posing a question broadly in this way invites *conversation*. So you reap the benefits not only of multiple perspectives, but also of a dialogue and interplay of these perspectives.

Target Direct Questions to Specific Individuals

Yet many questions are either too private or too specialized for wide broadcast. In these cases, you want to target a few particular and carefully selected individuals. When Ben and

I were selecting among publishers for this book, for example, we didn't post our questions to our entire networks online or send mass emails to everyone in our address books. Instead, we sought advice from just a handful of folks who had either published a book or worked in publishing—people who possessed the specialized, relevant expertise.

You probably instinctively do this already. You may have a go-to friend who is good at explaining what's really happening in the economy (as I have in Peter Thiel). Or you may know someone who's great at understanding people and emotions and whom you count on for relationship advice or navigating interpersonal challenges (as Ben has in Stephen Dodson). We all have certain people we call upon for advice or information on certain topics or issues, but not everyone knows who in their network to go to for intelligence on various career-related decisions.

One way to start thinking about this is to sort the people you know into three (at times overlapping) categories:

1. *Domain experts.* These are the pros, the people who really know the topic at hand. Got a question about negotiating your salary? Ask your lawyer friend who has negotiated a million contracts.

2. *People who know you well.* Your mother. Your childhood friend. These are the people who may not be up on the latest industry happenings, but they have a good sense of your priorities, personality, and personal history. They can help you unpack feelings of confusion and sometimes even intuit how you'll likely feel about various outcomes of your decision.

3. *Just really smart people.* These people may not be domain experts in the specific topic area and may not know you well. But occasionally sheer analytical horsepower can be useful. At the least, whatever a really smart outsider says stands a chance of being completely different from anything else you'll hear.

As a general rule, when you want information from your network, when facing a decision, *begin by asking domain experts, then talk to people with whom you have strong personal relationships.* If you're still not satisfied, or want yet another perspective, then turn to really smart outsiders. Iris Wong talked to her father only *after* talking to a friend with years of experience in a business similar to hers. If you want to break into the hospitality industry, for example, ping a few people in the industry (regardless of how well you know them) in order to get a sense of your overall options. You may need to ask for an introduction from someone in your network in order to get in front of the industry experts—refer back to Chapter 4 for more on your extended network. Then, confer with closer allies who know you well to help prioritize the options and figure out the best personal fit.

If you maintain a network that's both broad and deep, you'll have plenty of both types to talk to. Remember that breadth introduces acquaintances who hail from different industries, demographics, backgrounds, political orientations, and the like. Amid all that diversity (including second- or third-degree connections) there are bound to be experts in many different domains. With depth, you maintain a set of close relationships with people who know you well.

Online social networks facilitate this by keeping you up-to-date on whom you know and what *they* know, which allows you to target certain connections more efficiently. For example, on LinkedIn you can sort your connections to show everyone you know who works in a specific industry or lives in a specific region.

When we were thinking about whom we'd ask to read a draft of this book, the first thing we did was search our LinkedIn networks. I found domain experts I also knew professionally by searching my first-degree connections for the keyword "author." (Another reason why you should write a detailed professional profile: you're more likely to be found when people do keyword searches.) Separately, I browsed my "rockstar" tag, which showed all the people I had specially tagged as being supersmart (regardless of their background). Ben did similarly on his network, and of these folks, we asked a small set for their feedback.

Ask Good Questions

Charlene Begley ascended the ranks of GE for more than twenty years, rotating through positions in corporate auditing, aircraft engine design, appliances, and transportation locomotives. Now she's a senior executive at GE's corporate headquarters. "In all of these environments, you have to learn as much as you can as fast as you can, and you need to make an impact right away," says Begley, when asked how she's thrived in so many unimaginably diverse positions.

"The secret to this really isn't a secret: you have to ask a lot of questions."[5]

Asking a lot of good questions is the secret to network intelligence, too. It may sound obvious, but if you don't actually pose your inquiries in ways that generate useful answers, nothing else matters.

Here are some tips for asking better questions:

• *Converse, don't interrogate.* Spirited back-and-forth generates the most useful intelligence. If you're talking to a mentor or someone else obviously superior in status, it may be appropriate and expected for you to ask question after question. But when talking with allies and peers, offer thoughts of your own as a way of encouraging a real conversation. Give some intelligence to the other person and it will nudge them to reciprocate. So even though you want as much helpful information as possible, don't be a reporter and treat your peers as interviewees. Have an even, true exchange; in the long run, richer information will be exchanged.

• *Adjust the lens.* A simple example of the difference between a wide-lens question and a narrow-lens question is the difference between asking an architect, "How important is going to graduate school for someone interested in architecture?" versus "How highly rated is Cornell's graduate program in architecture?" The wide-lens question may elicit a long rant about how the person got screwed over by a pricey graduate program that didn't deliver the promised career boost. On the other hand, the narrow question invites specific, often factual answers about the specific area of inquiry—and nothing else:

"Yes, Cornell is in the top ten architecture schools." When you're trying to make a decision, ask wide questions to figure out the criteria you should be using; ask narrow questions to figure out which weight you should give to each. For example, ask primarily domain experts, "What should I be thinking about when assessing the pros and cons of this opportunity?" Then, once you've narrowed down your criteria, ask a more select group (including people you know well) for specific information about factors X and Y.

• *Frame and prime.* Countless studies show that the way an issue is framed or primed influences how that question will be answered. So to get the highest-quality intelligence you'll want to frame the same question in multiple ways. Ask someone, "What are the top three things you did right when you worked at the company I'm about to join?" Then ask the same person, "What three things did you *not* get to do at the company and wish you did?" You may well get a more useful answer about someone's experiences with the negative frame—there's something about reflecting on regret that leads to honest, useful insights. Another way to prime the answerer is to throw out a few sample answers to give a sense of the type of answer you're looking for. "What do you see as the pros and cons of architecture school? For example, maybe a pro is that I'll grow my network of architects?" By offering up the *kind* of answer that's helpful, you invite an answer of a similar level of specificity.

• *Follow up and probe.* It's rare you'll get a person's best intelligence with a single question. Follow up and probe on qualifying words. If someone says, "It's really risky to work at

Microsoft," continue with "What does 'risky' mean?" If that person says, "There's not a lot of job security," ask what "not a lot" means. Dig until a deeper answer takes shape. Some people hesitate to ask too many questions because they fear it will make them look ignorant. It won't. It'll make you look like a curious, intelligent person hungering for valuable information.

Finally, remember that if you're able to pose a very directed, detailed question, you're already advanced in your thinking and close to an answer. For thorny, big-picture anxieties it's sometimes hard to articulate a specific question to ask. Maybe there is something you're vaguely concerned with but you can't put it into words. *Something doesn't feel right at my job. What's going on?* Even if you can't translate into precise words the thing that's gnawing at you, your network can still play a valuable intelligence role, though it's a more involved process. For vague or nebulous concerns, engage people in person and try to tease out the issues over a long conversation.

Occasion Serendipity

As we wrote in Chapter 5, serendipity comes about when you're in motion, when you're *doing stuff*. Serendipitous network intelligence turns up in similar ways—when you're *engaging people*. If you're in touch and top of mind, someone may forward an email with information that's relevant just because they're thinking of you. And, you never know what useful nuggets a person might throw out at a party or over a casual lunch. Serendipitous intelligence is one reason why tech start-ups move to Silicon Valley despite fierce competition for talent, resources, and attention.

Just as there are things you can do to court serendipity, there are ways to court serendipitous intelligence. Keep a few general questions in your back pocket to ask people in these kinds of situations or settings. A back-pocket question could be as broad as "What's the most interesting thing you've learned over the past few months?" (the economist Tyler Cowen asks Ben this every time they see each other), or as targeted as "Have you come across any awesome entrepreneurs or start-ups that I should invest in?" (I ask this of anyone in the entrepreneurial ecosystem during casual conversation). You never know where these questions may lead—possibly somewhere interesting.

These days, more and more serendipitous network intelligence is emerging online. When you browse a connection's newsfeed on LinkedIn or Facebook, you aren't necessarily looking for anything in particular, but you may stumble upon an interesting article about your industry or see that a former coworker has moved to a company you want to work for or learn that a friend has started a business you want to partner with.

In addition, staying logged in to Amazon, LinkedIn, Yahoo, Facebook, Yelp, Google, and the other "dial tones" of the Internet, as Zynga CEO Mark Pincus calls them, can personalize your serendipitous intelligence. Land on CNN .com and you can pull up articles your Facebook friends have shared. Browse *Fortune* magazine's "100 Best Companies to Work For" list, and next to each company is a list of your LinkedIn connections out to the third degree who work there—making it easy to focus on companies where you already have a foot in the door. Instead of an anonymous editor or algorithm telling millions of readers what's important or relevant, the rise of a social web allows trusted connections to act as information curators.

Finally, pushing interesting information out to your network increases your chances of serendipitous intelligence. Post an article, email a quote, forward along a job offer, and in other ways share small gifts to your network. Your friends will appreciate it, and you will increase the chances that those same people respond in kind and send *you* intelligence later on.

SYNTHESIZE INFORMATION INTO ACTIONABLE INTELLIGENCE

After ten years in finance and international investment banking, Catherine Markwell wanted off the treadmill. The finance culture was such that the moment you finished a deal, you were supposed to hunger for the next one, and then the next one. It wasn't clear to her that all the dealmaking was improving the world. She wanted to do something more meaningful. A purposeful job is not an uncommon desire, but converting that feeling into something that pays the bills is more challenging. Catherine's friends encouraged her to take her business experience to the not-for-profit sector. She was intrigued, but leaving finance to enter a sector in which she had no full-time experience and sparse connections seemed daunting.

Many people in Catherine's position would have sat and stewed at this point. A lot of smart people are prone to over-analysis and tend to become paralyzed by indecision at this sort of juncture point. But Catherine knew enough to know it was an issue she couldn't process alone.

One of the first people she called was Hale Boggs, her lawyer from her banking days. Hale knew Catherine well. He knew she had big ambitions, but was at heart a careful person. So he advised her to get some experience by working at an existing not-for-profit before trying to start a new foundation that could succeed at the level to which she aspired. Catherine concurred, so she started looking at jobs at established organizations like the Red Cross.

At the same time, Hale introduced Catherine to friend and venture capitalist Tim Draper with the hope that Tim could identify local not-for-profit opportunities. Turned out Tim did indeed know of a good opportunity—his own organization. A couple years earlier, Tim had set up a small foundation called BizWorld in the bottom floor of his venture capital firm in Menlo Park. BizWorld aimed to spread the passion for entrepreneurship curriculum to elementary school students around the world. It was a powerful vision, but Tim didn't have time to run it. He wanted Catherine to become the foundation's chief executive officer.

Catherine loved the concept—business, personal finance, and entrepreneurship were all topics she was passionate about. Plus, heading up a small foundation already in existence would mean she could have the responsibility she'd envisioned when she'd thought about starting her own organization, while learning from an operation that was already in place. There was one potential hitch. She had to really gel with the sole founder and funder: Tim.

Vetting, reference checking, and obtaining in-depth color about another person is something entrepreneurs do every time they make a new hire, and it's something every professional does many, many times in his or her career. When you operate within a network, you even have the ability to do the same reference checks on people you're thinking about going to work *for,* i.e., a potential boss. Whether you're reference-checking bosses, organizations, possible coworkers, or people you're tasked to hire, one source of information trumps all others: *other people.* People can offer honest, nuanced analyses of competency and character; things that résumés and Google searches and Wikipedia pages simply can't. Catherine knew this, which is why she tapped her network to learn as much as she could about Tim. She emailed entrepreneurs, other VCs, and service providers in Silicon Valley—experts in Tim's field. She asked people who knew him well and people who didn't know him well. She asked people she suspected would say nice things about Tim, yet she also sought out people she believed would be more critical. "There wasn't much online about Tim at the time," says Catherine, explaining her network intelligence-gathering process. "Of the stuff written on him in the press, there wasn't the kind of personal depth that I was looking for. So

I called and emailed lots of different people with the same questions."

The signals relayed back from her network made her positive on Tim and positive on the BizWorld opportunity. So she decided to join BizWorld as its director in March 2003. She effectively relaunched the foundation, clarified its mission, and added programming and staff. Almost a decade later, she's still happily at BizWorld, and her partnership with Tim remains strong. Catherine feels like she's making more of a difference in the world than she ever did as a banker.

The interesting thing about this story is that Catherine would never have come to the decision that she did if she hadn't *synthesized* the information from her multiple sources. Had she spoken only to Hale Boggs, she would probably have ended up working at the Red Cross. Had she not gathered intelligence on Tim Draper, she might have concluded that working so closely with a total stranger was too big of a risk. But when she put all the various streams of information she received together, it revealed a fuller picture—a picture that ultimately led her to the right decision.

∘ ∘ •

Remember that NOAA scientists cannot predict a tsunami based on a single sensor in the ocean. In order to come to a judgment, they (1) collect readings from *multiple* sensors dispersed throughout the Atlantic and Pacific Oceans, (2) analyze each piece of information that comes in, and (3) synthesize the various streams of data to understand how the different pieces fit together.

So far we've talked about the first step—pulling information from multiple people in your network. Once you have gathered information, the next step is to analyze the validity, helpfulness, and relevance of what each person has said. Remember that *everyone* has biases—even your parents or best friend. It's not that they are trying to manipulate you. It's just the nature of being a human with personal experiences and self-interests. Bias can be obvious or nonobvious, conscious or subconscious. A friend who stands to earn a bonus for referring new hires at his company may enthusiastically encourage you to apply for a job there—a bias that is transparent and relatively harmless. Friends who adamantly encourage the career choices that just happen to be the same ones they have made—this is a more hidden bias that you and they may not be aware of, and so it's a bit more dangerous. As you pull information and advice from various sources, think about how the person's personal goals, ambitions, and experience might have colored their position. Bias is not reason to dismiss information or advice altogether; just account for it in your analysis (as Iris Wong did when she questioned whether to interpret her coworkers' advice as rational cynicism or overheated anxiety).

Synthesis is the important final step. If you don't step back and take in the big picture of all you've learned, it will feel like you're worming your way through a cocktail party hearing bits and pieces of several different conversations but not able to make out anything of substance. Synthesizing what you learn involves reconciling contradictory advice and information (which is inevitable if you're pulling multiple streams from diverse people), ignoring information you believe is completely off base, and weighing each person's information differently. This is a complex cognitive process. For now, we'll just say that when it comes to intelligence, *good synthesis is what makes the whole worth more than the sum of the parts.*

When Catherine Markwell gathered feedback from her network on how to start a not-for-profit, she was told she ought to work at an established foundation before heading up her own. It was sound advice and she planned on following it. Then she got introduced (through her network) to an opportunity to relaunch an existing foundation in its infancy. She wouldn't be gaining experience at an established entity like the Red Cross, as her trusted friend had advised her. Yet she *would* be breaking into the not-for-profit world with a position offering close to the same control she would have if she had started the organization. The original piece of advice to work at a Red Cross first wasn't completely ignored. It was simply placed in context alongside her other opportunities—it was stitched together with other information. That's synthesis.

*   *   ●

Acquiring good network intelligence is hard. Anyone can read a book or blog. Anybody can talk to random people around the office or neighborhood. It's harder to identify the right people to talk to on different issues, ask these people questions that invite maximally useful answers, and synthesize points into something meaningful. Network intelligence is the advanced game: if you do it well, it'll give you a competitive edge.

In the end, only you can make the final judgment call on

whether an opportunity is worth it, whether pivoting to Plan B is necessary, whether a certain individual is a trusted ally— whether any decision is right for you. I^{We} means your network can help you decide on a direction and then help you move quickly, but only you can drive the process forward.

INVEST IN YOURSELF

In the next day:

• Adjust your LinkedIn newsfeed to make sure it's showing the information that's most helpful. Select which types of updates you want to see from your network. Go into Signal (linkedin.com/signal) and save search queries on relevant topics.

• If you're using Twitter, are you following the people you should be following? Check your list, and add or remove as necessary.

In the next week:

• Map out whom you trust on different topics. Sort your connections into domain experts, people who know you well, and people who may not have specific expertise but are just smart in general. Who's your go-to person on technology? Whom would you approach to discuss an interpersonal issue you're having with a coworker?

• Make a list of the two to three top issues you're thinking about, and keep questions about those issues in your back pocket so you can raise them in conversation.

• Post one article each week to an email list, blog, Twitter followers, or your LinkedIn connections or Facebook friends. Remember that pushing interesting information out to your network increases the chances that other people will send you valuable information.

In the next month:

• Schedule three lunch dates to take place in upcoming weeks: one with a person a few rungs ahead of you in your industry; one with an old friend you haven't seen in a while; and one with a person from an adjacent industry whose career you admire. Do this even if you aren't currently facing a pressing career question or challenge. Probe on general, time-insensitive topics. Engaged conversation can sometimes lead to serendipitous intelligence.

• Become a go-to person for *other* people in your network on certain topics. Make known to your connections your interests and skills by writing blog posts and emails, or setting up discussion groups. When people come to you for intelligence, you are simultaneously acquiring intelligence from them.

Conclusion

You were born an entrepreneur.

However, that doesn't guarantee you will live like one. Instincts need nurturing. Potential needs realizing. You can take control of your life and apply entrepreneurial skills to whatever work you do—the question is, *will you*?

The modern world demands it. We live in an interconnected, fast-moving, and competitive economy. Constant change and uncertainty make any traditional career strategy ineffective. The career escalator is permanently jammed. The employer-employee pact is dissolving. Competition for opportunity is fierce.

Remember that the "You" in *Start-Up of You* is both singular and plural. While we've offered a number of individual strategies for navigating the new realities, your network amplifies them: the power of I^{We} is what allows you to survive and thrive. Globally competitive professionals work within strong networks. As we discussed, allies help you develop a competitive advantage, do ABZ planning, pursue breakout opportunities, take intelligent risks, and tap network intelligence. You absolutely need to take control of *your* career, but you also need to invest in the careers of others in your network who will help you and whom you will help in turn.

In addition to you and the network around you, there's a broader environment that shapes your career potential: the nature of the *society* you live in. If the local culture, institutions, and population do not engender an entrepreneurial life, the *Start-Up of You* strategies yield only a small portion of their real potential.

An entrepreneur who is trying to build a business in an unhealthy society is like a seed in a pot that never gets watered: no matter how talented that entrepreneur, his business cannot flourish. As Warren Buffett says, "If you stick me down in the middle of Bangladesh or Peru or someplace, you find out how much this talent is going to produce in the wrong kind of soil." Berkshire Hathaway was founded in America because there's greater business opportunity in a country with effective institutions, rule of law, trust, and a culture that accepts risk-taking, among other intangible qualities. And, when a Warren Buffett has the opportunity to flourish, everyone in society benefits. The soil gains nutrients to nourish the seeds of other people's creativity. This is why enlightened for-profit companies align their for-profit business objectives with desirable social outcomes. It's also why they allocate time and money to directly help the communities in which they operate. At LinkedIn, employees get paid days off to volunteer at local not-for-profits. These charitable endeavors do good *and* help the bottom line. They strengthen the company's connection both with current or prospective customers and with its employees.

The health of a society shapes the outcomes for individual professionals in a similar fashion. It's difficult to build a remarkable career if the society you live in features extreme poverty, poor services and infrastructure, or low levels of trust. For one thing, there are fewer good jobs in a place with disrepair like Detroit. But this goes beyond where there are the most job openings. In healthy societies, people are more likely to share information, join groups, and collaborate on projects together—all activities that eventually magnify career opportunities, both for you and for the people who come after you.

Think carefully about where you choose to live and work. Then commit to improving whatever community you do live in. You don't have to be Mother Teresa. Investing in society can be as simple as doing something once a year that's not directly for you. Do something that's in line with your values and aspirations and that preferably leverages your unique soft and hard assets—in other words, make use of your competitive advantages. Better still, involve yourself in organizations that try to systemically improve society at a massive scale. Kiva.org enables global micro-lending to alleviate poverty; Endeavor.org promotes entrepreneurship in developing markets; Start-Up America helps support entrepreneurs across the U.S. I'm on the boards of all three.

For Ben and me, this book is one of our gifts back to society. We think the tools in this book can improve both your life and society. Sometimes giving back can be simply spreading ideas that matter.

Along the way, of course, the praise from others may make you feel good about yourself, just like companies enjoy press for their philanthropy. But giving back means much more: you enrich the soil for future generations, as prior generations did for you. It's the right thing to do.

Invest in yourself, invest in your network, *and* invest in society. When you invest in all three, you have the best shot at reaching your highest professional potential. As important, you also have the best shot at changing the world.

*   *   *

One final point. Books and speeches and articles on entrepreneurship proclaim to impart the top rules of the trade. The irony is that the extraordinary entrepreneurs tend to challenge the rules and partially ignore the "experts"—they come up with their own principles, their own rules of thumb. After all, the way you achieve differentiation in the market is by *not* doing what everyone else is doing.

There's a similar bulge of career books filled with "expert" rules. Of course, we believe the vast majority of professionals do not grasp what it means to run a career like a start-up venture; we believe implementing the strategies discussed in these pages *will* give you an edge. But think of them as guidelines, not rules of nature. Sometimes in order to make something work, you will drive over the guardrail of one of these rules. Sometimes you evolve new rules in order to stay ahead of the competition. One of the key messages we hope you've taken away from this book is that you are changing, the people around you are changing, and the broader world is changing—so it's inevitable the playbook will evolve and adapt.

So start tapping into your network. Start investing in skills. Start taking intelligent risks. Start pursuing breakout opportunities. But most of all, start forging your own differentiated career plans; start adapting these rules to your own adaptive life.

For life in permanent beta, the trick is to never stop starting.

The start-up is you.

—Reid and Ben
www.startupofyou.com/start

Connect with Us

On the book's website, www.startupofyou.com, you'll find more information and advanced strategies for how to invest in yourself, strengthen your network, and transform your career. You'll also be able to connect with other professionals, also in permanent beta, who will help you move from ideas to action, from knowledge to implementation.

* * *

Some of the exclusive online content includes:

1. A free PDF with advanced techniques for using LinkedIn to implement some of the strategies in this book.

2. Video interviews with Sheryl Sandberg, Mark Pincus, Joi Ito, and other top executives from different fields reflecting on their careers and sharing lessons learned.

3. An executive summary of *The Start-Up of You*—all the key points summarized and formatted in a way that's easily shareable. (It makes a good "small gift" to someone in your network!)

On Twitter, you can find us at @startupofyou. Append the hashtag **#startYOU** to your tweets about ABZ planning, networks, competitive advantage, or any other idea from the book. We'll reply to and promote the best questions, comments, or ideas that circulate on Twitter.

See you online!

Further Reading

Below is more information on the books referenced in the earlier chapters, as well as a few additional recommendations on related themes. On our website, we link to each of these books, as well as to numerous other articles, blogs, Twitter feeds, and more.

Free Agent Nation: The Future of Working for Yourself
By Daniel H. Pink

In 2002, Pink made popular the phrase "free agent" to describe the self-employment phenomenon in the United States. At the time, Pink estimated that one-quarter to one-third of American workers worked as independent contractors. He explores their attitudes toward autonomy, informal networks, self-constructed safety nets, and more. The *mentality* of the self-employed people Pink profiles is relevant to anyone who wants to think more like an entrepreneur.

The Brand You 50: Or, Fifty Ways to Transform Yourself from an "Employee" into a Brand That Shouts Distinction, Commitment, and Passion!
By Tom Peters

This is the book version of Tom Peters's famous 1997 article in *Fast Company* titled "The Brand Called You." Peters pioneered the idea of "You, Inc." He says you should think about what makes you stand out and then aggressively promote those distinctive skills, accomplishments, and passions—which together make up your personal brand—just like a company would promote its products and services.

Working Identity: Unconventional Strategies for Reinventing Your Career
By Herminia Ibarra

This is a great book on career reinvention and transition. A professor of organizational behavior at INSEAD, Ibarra tells the stories of men and women who pivoted into new industries. She observes how difficult it is to shed your old identity and create a new one. She stresses the importance of experimentation. And she hammers home the idea that there is no "one true self" that can be discovered.

Only the Paranoid Survive: How to Exploit the Crisis Points That Challenge Every Business
By Andrew S. Grove

Intel cofounder Andy Grove introduces the concept of Strategic Inflection Points: crucial moments in the life of a company where the actions taken will determine whether the company survives massive environmental change and emerges stronger than ever, or whether it declines dramatically. Grove makes the case for staying in front of change. The most recent edition of the book contains an extra chapter on career inflection points, which is quite useful.

One Person/Multiple Careers: A New Model for Work/ Life Success
By Marci Alboher

Marci says you can successfully weave together seemingly different career interests into one unified whole—all at once. You don't have work in one industry for a long time and then make a frightening leap to another. Marci interviews lawyers/chefs, journalists/doctors, and others in a "slash career." The book presents a whole new way to think about combining passions.

Different: Escaping the Competitive Herd
By Youngme Moon

Moon argues that to have a true competitive advantage in today's business world means that a company must be fundamentally different from the outset. It can't bolt on differentiators after the fact. Recommended reading to explore the concept of competitive advantage in more detail.

Your Career Game: How Game Theory Can Help You Achieve Your Professional Goals
By Nathan Bennett and Stephen A. Miles

This is practical career advice in a style that's unusually substantive and dense. Bennett and Miles interview top executives about their careers and derive principles of success. They stress "career agility" and write thoughtfully on creating differentiation as a professional.

The Invention of Air: A Story About Science, Faith, Revolution and the Birth of America
By Steven Johnson

A story about the life and times of Joseph Priestley, who was the first person to discover oxygen and the first person to realize that plants were also creating it. Johnson shows that the "discovery" of oxygen was not the result of a single eureka moment but rather the culmination of many experiences and influences over an extended period of time. The discussion of Priestley's networks and relationships is particularly relevant to career networks and relationships.

Where Good Ideas Come From: The Natural History of Innovation
By Steven Johnson

Johnson explains the environmental causes of innovation, including the role of open networks, collaboration, serendipity, adjacent niches, and many other concepts relevant to fostering breakout career opportunities. An excellent analysis.

The Power of Pull: How Small Moves, Smartly Made, Can Set Big Things in Action
By John Hagel III, John Seely Brown, and Lang Davison

The authors say the twenty-first-century model of knowledge acquisition is about "pulling" information in from dynamic "knowledge flows." By placing the social network at the center of information gathering and opportunity flow, the book complements well our discussion of serendipity and network intelligence.

Little Bets: How Breakthrough Ideas Emerge from Small Discoveries

By Peter Sims

Adapt: Why Success Always Starts with Failure

By Tim Harford

Peter and Tim each argue for an experimental approach to business, politics, and life. Rather than betting big on a large endeavor that takes a long time to pay off, companies—and individuals—should take many small risks and see which ones turn out okay. Eric Schmidt of Google calls this philosophy "the most at-bats per unit of time."

The Happiness Hypothesis: Finding Modern Truth in Ancient Wisdom

By Jonathan Haidt

Haidt, a psychology professor at the University of Virginia, presents fascinating insights from the latest research on happiness. In one chapter, he writes about how humans are more focused on avoiding risk than seizing the upside, which is relevant to our discussion of risks and opportunities.

Streetlights and Shadows: Searching for the Keys to Adaptive Decision Making

By Gary Klein

An original and counterintuitive set of ideas on how to make better decisions. Unlike many books on decision-making, Klein assumes you have incomplete information and high levels of uncertainty—in other words, he assumes you live in the real world, not an academic lab.

Connected: The Surprising Power of Our Social Networks and How They Shape Our Lives
By Nicholas Christakis and James Fowler

Drawing on extensive (if not completely proven) research, social scientists Christakis and Fowler argue that connections up to three degrees away from us have a profound effect on our mind and body. Christakis and Fowler say that we are very much the company we keep—out to the third degree.

Working Together: Why Great Partnerships Succeed
By Michael D. Eisner with Aaron Cohen

Eisner, former CEO of Disney, writes about ten notable partnerships. Susan Feniger and Mary Sue Milliken are featured in the book, as are Brian Grazer and Ron Howard, Warren Buffett and Charlie Munger, Bill Gates and Melinda Gates, and others. These inspiring stories show the power of alliance.

Pull: Networking and Success Since Benjamin Franklin
By Pamela Walker Laird

Laird demolishes the idea of the "self-made man" and adds historical depth to the idea of I^{We}. A good account of how famous figures like Ben Franklin operated within a web of social support.

Superconnect: The Power of Networks and the Strength of Weak Links
By Richard Koch and Greg Lockwood

An in-depth exploration of "weak ties," including a review of the academic studies that coined the term, and what professionals need to know about how weak ties function in a social network.

The Future Arrived Yesterday: The Rise of the Protean Corporation and What It Means for You
By Michael Malone

What does a company of the future look like? Michael says it's a "protean corporation," one that can constantly adapt to new challenges by restructuring itself instantly. Organizations like Wikipedia and Google fit this mold. This book is an intriguing portrait of tomorrow's workplace.

Acknowledgments

It takes a network to write a book. We extend a huge thanks to Talia Krohn for her fantastic job editing the book and for passionately championing the project for more than a year. Lisa DiMona offered wise counsel and encouragement from the very beginning. Brett Bolkowy assisted in researching and refining the book's ideas and contributed essential organizational support. Peter Economy and Josh Mitrani provided research and editorial support. Von Glitschka did the chapter illustrations.

* * *

I've had the joy and delight of working with some of my close network on this book. I unfortunately missed working with other key people in my network on this project due to logistical constraints. So it feels right to thank all of my network, because they all helped develop the ideas herein. In particular, I'd like to call out three of my teachers whose early gifts of time and insight changed my life: Lisa Cox and Tom Wessells from the Putney School, who set me on my initial path of being a public intellectual, and Jonathan Reider at Stanford University, who amplified that path.

—RGH

• • ●

I'm grateful to the many people who supported me in this project. A special tip of the hat to Jessie Young, Stephen Dodson, Chris Yeh, and Cal Newport for going beyond the call of duty. And heartfelt thanks to my parents for everything they do.

—BTC

Notes

Chapter 1

1. "Centuries of immigrants" and "risked everything" were inspired by Barack Obama's 2011 State of the Union address. "Obama's Second State of the Union (Text)," *New York Times*, January 25, 2011, http://www.nytimes.com/2011/01/26/us/politics/26obama-text.html?_r=1&sq=obama%20state%20union&st=cse&scp=2&pagewanted=all

2. Ronald Brownstein, "Children of the Great Recession," *The Atlantic*, May 5, 2010, http://www.theatlantic.com/special-report/the-next-economy/archive/2010/05/children-of-the-great-recession/56248/

3. Ibid.

4. The mother of all safety nets, Social Security is supposed to be funded by the federal government . . . a government that happens to be trillions of dollars in debt. If you're in your twenties or thirties today, by the time you retire you'll likely collect at least 25 percent less in cash than your parents did. (More-draconian analysts predict a young person today will get nothing.) Consider the Social Security tax that comes out of your paycheck like you would a loan to a second cousin who has a drug problem—you might get paid back, but don't count on it.

5. "Cost-Cutting Strategies in the Downturn: A Delicate Balancing Act," May 2009, http://www.towerswatson.com/assets/pdf/610/CostCutting-RB_12-29-09.pdf

6. Andy Kessler, "Is Your Job an Endangered Species?" *Wall Street Journal,* February 17, 2011, http://online.wsj.com/article/SB10001424052748703439504576116340050218236.html

7. See the links in Will Wilkinson's discussion, "Are ATMs Stealing Jobs?" *The Economist,* June 15, 2011, http://www.economist.com/blogs/democracyinamerica/2011/06/technology-and-unemployment

8. Alex Taylor III, *Sixty to Zero* (New Haven: Yale University Press, 2011), 14.

9. "Population of the 20 Largest US Cities, 1900–2005," *Information Please,* http://www.infoplease.com/ipa/A0922422.html

10. "Address in Detroit at the Celebration of the City's 250th Anniversary," July 28, 1951, in *Public Papers of the Presidents of the United States: Harry S. Truman, 1951: Containing the Public Messages, Speeches, and Statements of the President, January 1 to December 31, 1951* (Washington, DC: General Services Administration, National Archives and Records Service, Office of the Federal Register, 1965), 429.

11. Andrew Malcolm, "Obama Takes the Wheel from Detroit," *Los Angeles Times,* March 30, 2009, http://latimesblogs.latimes.com/washington/2009/03/obama-to-detroi.html

12. Statistics from Charlie LeDuff, "What Killed Aiyana Stanley-Jones?" *Mother Jones* (November/December 2010), http://motherjones.com/print/79151

13. John Hagel III, John Seely Brown, Duleesha Kulasooriya, and Dan Elbert, "Measuring the Forces of Long-term

Change: The 2010 Shift Index," Deloitte Center for the Edge (2010), 2, http://www.deloitte.com/assets/Dcom-UnitedStates/Local%20Assets/Documents/TMT_us_tmt/Shift%20Index%202010/us_tmt_si_shift%20Index2010_110310.pdf

14. Reed Hastings, as told to Amy Zipkin, "Out of Africa, Onto the Web," *New York Times*, December 17, 2006, http://www.nytimes.com/2006/12/17/jobs/17boss.html

15. Rick Newman, "How Netflix (and Blockbuster) Killed Blockbuster," *U.S. News & World Report*, September 23, 2010, http://money.usnews.com/money/blogs/flowchart/2010/9/23/how-netflix-and-blockbuster-killed-blockbuster.html

16. Greg Sandoval, "Blockbuster Laughed at Netflix Partnership Offer," CNET *News,* December 9, 2010, http://news.cnet.com/8301-31001_3-20025235-261.html

17. "Netflix Opens New Shipping Center; Lakeland Facility Expands One-Day Delivery to Central Florida," PR Newswire, January 15, 2004, http://www.highbeam.com/doc/1G1-131553666.html

18. Company 2009 10-K SEC filings.

19. Jeffrey Bezos, letter to shareholders, April 2010, http://phx.corporate-ir.net/External.File?item=UGFyZW50SUQ9Mzc2NjQ0fENoaWxkSUQ9Mzc1Mjc5fFR5cGU9MQ==&t=1

20. Jeffrey Pfeffer, *Power: Why Some People Have It—And Others Don't* (New York: HarperBusiness, 2010), 49.

Chapter 2

1. John Hagel III, John Seely Brown, and Lang Davison, *The Power of Pull: How Small Moves, Smartly Made, Can Set Big Things in Motion* (New York: Basic Books, 2010), 12.

2. The phrase "overcome by sameness" is inspired by Youngme Moon's analysis of differentiation in her book *Difference*, Kindle edition, location 156.

3. See video of Chris Sacca and Kevin Rose discussing this point: http://vimeo.com/26021720

4. Herminia Ibarra, *Working Identity: Unconventional Strategies for Reinventing Your Career* (Boston, MA: Harvard Business School Press, 2004), 35.

5. http://www.mhhe.com/business/management/thompson/11e/case/starbucks.html

6. http://www.jetblue.com/about/ourcompany/flightlog/index.html

Chapter 3

1. Richard N. Bolles, *What Color Is Your Parachute?* 2011 Edition (New York: Ten Speed Press, 2011), 28.

2. Kevin Conley, "Sheryl Sandberg: What She Saw at the Revolution," *Vogue*, May 2010, http://www.vogue.com/magazine/article/sheryl-sandberg-what-she-saw-at-the-revolution/

3. Ken Auletta, "A Woman's Place: Can Sheryl Sandberg Upend Silicon Valley's Male-Dominated Culture?" *The New Yorker*, July 11, 2011, http://www.newyorker.com/reporting/2011/07/11/110711fa_fact_auletta?currentPage=all

4. http://www.businessweek.com/bwdaily/dnflash/content/mar2009/db20090316_630496.htm

5. See Jason Del Rey, "The Art of the Pivot," *Inc.*, February 1, 2011, http://www.inc.com/magazine/20110201/the-art-of-the-pivot.html

6. Andrew S. Grove, *Only the Paranoid Survive: How to Exploit the Crisis Points That Challenge Every Company* (New York: Crown Business, 1999), 189.

Chapter 4

1. Adrian Wooldridge, "The Silence of Mammon: Business People Should Stand Up for Themselves," *The Economist,* December 17, 2009, http://www.economist.com/node/15125372?story_id=15125372

2. Nicholas Christakis and James Fowler, *Connected: The Surprising Power of Our Social Networks and How They Shape Our Lives* (New York: Little, Brown and Company, 2009), 22.

3. Pamela Walker Laird, *Pull: Networking and Success Since Benjamin Franklin* (Cambridge, MA: Harvard University Press, 2007), 11.

4. Jeff Atwood, "The Bad Apple: Group Poison," *Coding Horror: Programming and Human Factors* (blog), February 19, 2009, http://www.codinghorror.com/blog/2009/02/the-bad-apple-group-poison.html

5. Paul Graham, "Why Smart People Have Bad Ideas," *PaulGraham.com* (blog), April 2005, http://www.paulgraham.com/bronze.html

6. David Foster Wallace, *This Is Water: Some Thoughts, Delivered on a Significant Occasion, About Living a Compassionate Life* (New York: Little, Brown, 2009), 39–40.

7. Neil Rackham and John Carlisle, "The Effective Negotiator, Part I: The Behaviour of Successful Negotiators," *Journal of European Industrial Training* 2, no. 6 (1978): 6–11, doi:10.1108/eb002297

8. Edward O. Laumann, John H. Gagnon, Robert T. Michael, and Stuart Michaels, *The Social Organization of Sexuality: Sexual Practices in the United States* (Chicago: University of Chicago Press, 1994).

9. David Brooks, *The Social Animal* (New York: Random House, 2011), 155.

10. How is he defining *weak tie*? In the study, he uses frequency of contact as a proxy for how strong the relationship is. This is an imperfect measure: you may see your secretary or the doorman every day, but that does not make him a strong tie. Granovetter acknowledged that measuring the strength of a relationship is a broader "combination of the amount of time, emotional intensity, the intimacy (mutual confiding), and the reciprocal services which characterize the tie." Subsequent research affirmed Granovetter's original conclusion even while measuring the strength of ties with more holistic criteria. See Granovetter's "The Strength of Weak Ties: A Network Theory Revisited," *Sociological Theory* 1 (1983): 201–33.

11. Mark S. Granovetter, "The Strength of Weak Ties," *American Journal of Sociology* 78, no. 6 (1973): 1371.

12. Ibid., 1362.

13. Herminia Ibarra, *Working Identity* (Cambridge, MA: Harvard Business School Press, 1994): 113.

14. See Dunbar's book *How Many Friends Does One Person Need?* (Cambridge, MA: Harvard University Press, 2010), as well as the Wikipedia entry for Dunbar's Number, http://en.wikipedia.org/wiki/Dunbar's_number. Also see Christopher Allen's nuanced parsing of the concept, "The Dunbar Number as a Limit to Group Sizes," *Life with Alacrity* (blog), March 10, 2004, http://www.lifewithalacrity.com/2004/03/the_dunbar_numb.html

15. Jeffrey Travers and Stanley Milgram, "An Experimental Study in the Small World Problem," *Sociometry* 35, no. 4 (1969): 425–43, doi:10.1109/TIT.2010.2054490

16. Hazer Inaltekin, Mung Chiang, and H. Vincent Poor, "Average Message Delivery Time for Small-world Networks in the Continuum Limit," *IEEE Transactions on Information Theory* 56, no. 9 (2010), 4447–70, doi:10.1109/TIT.2010.2054490

17. http://blog.okcupid.com/index.php/online-dating-advice-exactly-what-to-say-in-a-first-message/

18. Brian Uzzi and Jarrett Spiro, "Collaboration and Creativity: The Small World Problem," *American Journal of Sociology* 111, no. 2 (2005), 447–504. doi: 10.1086/432782

19. Nicholas Christakis and James Fowler, *Connected: The Surprising Power of Our Social Networks and How They Shape Our Lives* (New York: Little, Brown and Company, 2009): Kindle Location 2691.

20. See Stowe Boyd's blog post (and the comments section) for more on this theme: http://www.stoweboyd.com/post/756220523/its-betweenness-that-matters-not-your-eigenvalue-the

Chapter 5

1. Kimberly Potts, *George Clooney: The Last Great Movie Star* (New York: Applause Theatre & Cinema Books, 2007), 50.

2. James H. Austin, *Chase, Chance and Creativity: The Lucky Art of Novelty* (Cambridge, MA: Harvard University Press, 2003), 69.

3. A paraphrased sentence from James Austin.

4. Bo Peabody, *Lucky or Smart?: Secrets to an Entrepreneurial Life* (New York: Random House, 2004).

5. Steven Johnson, *The Invention of Air: A Story of Science, Faith, Revolution and the Birth of America* (New York: Riverhead Books, 2008), 53.

6. Ibid.

7. Pamela Walker Laird, *Pull: Networking and Success Since Benjamin Franklin* (Cambridge, MA, Harvard University Press, 2007), 88.

8. AnnaLee Saxenian, *Regional Advantage: Culture and Competition in Silicon Valley and Route 128* (Cambridge, MA: Harvard University Press, 1994), 34.

9. Michael Eisner and Aaron D. Cohen, *Working Together: Why Great Partnerships Succeed* (New York: Harper Business, 2010), 202.

10. Nicholas Carlson, "Jeff Bezos: Here's Why He Won," *Business Insider,* May 16, 2011, http://www.businessinsider.com/jeff-bezos-visionary-2011-4#ixzz1NsYA4QfS

11. Claire Cain Miller, "How Pandora Slipped Past the Junkyard," *New York Times,* March 7, 2010, http://dealbook.nytimes.com/2010/03/08/how-pandora-slipped-past-the-junkyard

Chapter 6

1. Reannon Muth, "Are Risk-Takers a Dying Breed?" *Matador,* June 13, 2010, http://matadornetwork.com/bnt/are-risk-takers-a-dying-breed/

2. Jonathan Haidt, *The Happiness Hypothesis: Finding Modern Truth in Ancient Wisdom* (New York: Basic Books, 2006), 29.

3. Anthony Iaquinto and Stephen Spinelli Jr., *Never Bet the Farm: How Entrepreneurs Take Risks, Make Decisions—and How You Can, Too* (San Francisco: Jossey-Bass, 2006), 78.

4. Stephen H. Shore and Raven Saks, "Risk and Career Choice," *Advances in Economic Analysis and Policy* 5, no. 1 (2005), http://www.bepress.com/bejeap/advances/vol5/iss1/art7

5. Nassim Taleb, *The Black Swan: The Impact of the Highly Improbable* (New York: Random House, 2010), 204.

6. Joshua Cooper Ramo, *The Age of the Unthinkable: Why the New World Disorder Constantly Surprises Us and What We Can Do About It* (New York: Back Bay Books, 2010), 181.

7. Ibid.

8. Aaron B. Wildavsky, *Searching for Safety* (Piscataway, NJ: Transaction Publishers, 2004), 98.

Chapter 7

1. Bill Gates, *Business @ the Speed of Thought: Using a Digital Nervous Sysem* (New York: Warner Books, 1999), 3.

2. Ken Auletta, "A Woman's Place: Can Sheryl Sandberg Upend Silicon Valley's Male-Dominated Culture?" *The New Yorker,* July 11, 2011, http://www.newyorker.com/reporting/2011/07/11/110711fa_fact_auletta?currentPage=all

3. Hagit Limor, "Anatomy of a Tsunami from the Center That Warned the World," *KY Post,* March 18, 2011, http://www.kypost.com/dpps/news/world/anatomy-of-a-tsunami-from-the-center-that-warned-the-world_6179439

4. "Report: Hawaii Tsunami Damage at $30.6M," *Pacific Business News,* March 24, 2011, http://www.bizjournals.com/

pacific/news/2011/03/24/report-hawaii-tsunami-damage-at
-306m.html

5. Nathan Bennett and Stephen Miles, *Your Career Game: How Game Theory Can Help You Achieve Your Professional Goals* (Stanford, CA: Stanford University Press, 2010), 16.

Index